1 'O' Trouble!

Circle the things that have the short 'O' sound.

2 The Red Fruit

Colour all the fruits that are red in colour.

3 Two in One

Sometimes two words join together to become a meaningful word, these are called compound words. Find the two words that make up each of these words.

   Football   = _____ + _____

   Grasshopper = _____ + _____

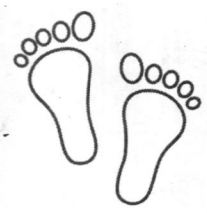   Footprints = _____ + _____

   Butterflies = _____ + _____

   Moonlight   = _____ + _____

   Saucepan   = _____ + _____

Date: _____   Teacher's Signature: _____

4 Party Time

How will you describe the picture given below?

Occasion: _____

Caption: _____

Now, use your imagination to colour the picture.

Date: _____ Teacher's Signature: _____

5 House of Words

Build a word house and create new words inside it.
Psst: Get hints from the Help Box to create new words.

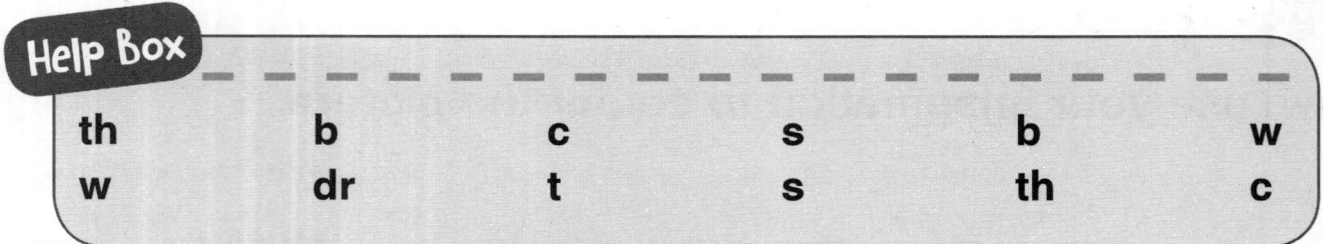

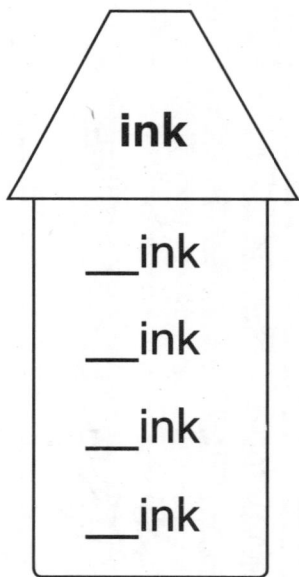

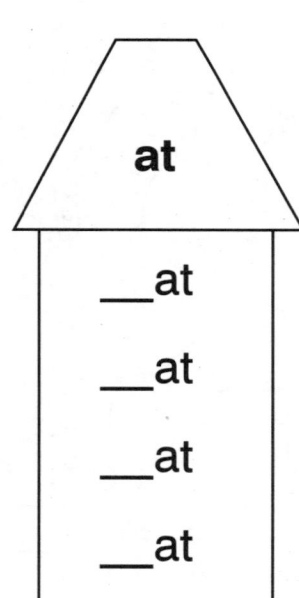

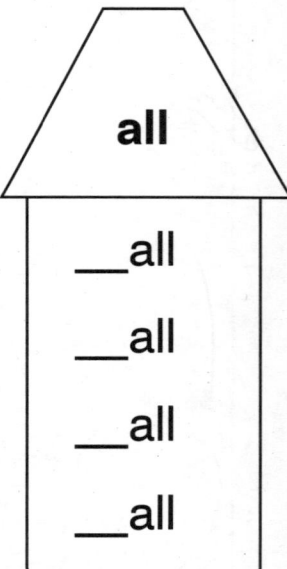

Missing Pair

Find the missing pair of letters from the Help Box and complete the words.

Help Box: sp   bl   fl   tr   gl   sk   br   sc   st

 __ __ oon

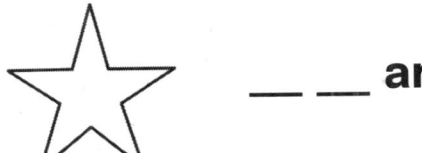 __ __ ar

 __ __ ick

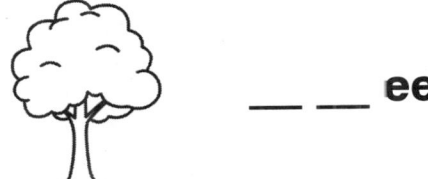 __ __ ee

 __ __ arf

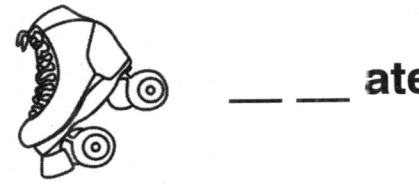 __ __ ate

 __ __ obe

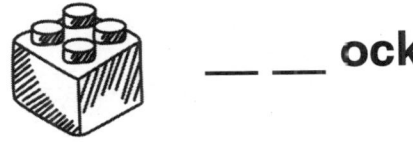 __ __ ock

 __ __ ower

1 What's That?

Identify the pictures given below. Write their name in the blank spaces.

_____

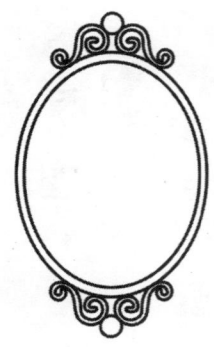
_____

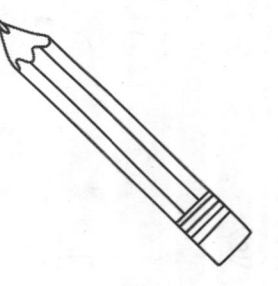
_____

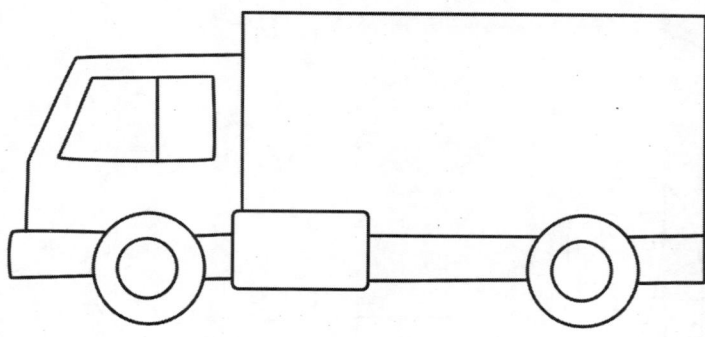
_____

_____

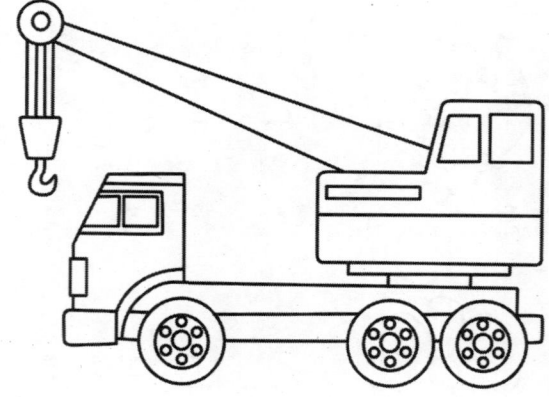
_____

Date: _____

Teacher's Signature: _____

8 The Last Two

Match the following to complete the words. One of them has been done for you.

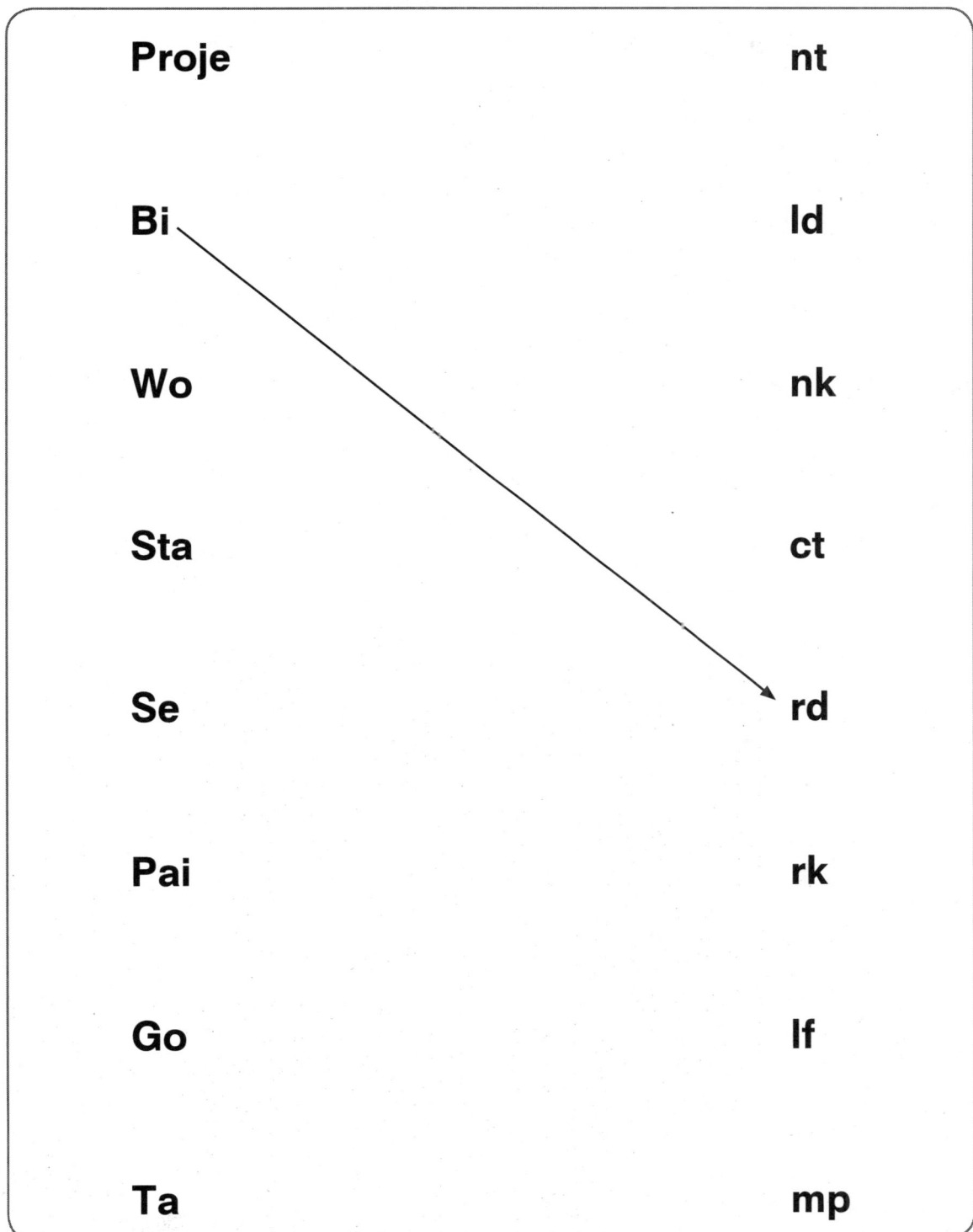

Proje	nt
Bi	ld
Wo	nk
Sta	ct
Se	rd
Pai	rk
Go	lf
Ta	mp

9 Fill in the Blanks

Choose the correct word from the Help Box to fill in the blanks.

Help Box

bat   cat   rats   fat

This is a _____.

This is his _____.

His cat is very _____ and

loves to eat _____.

Date: _____   Teacher's Signature: _____

10 We Belong Together

Which subject do the pictures belong to? Circle the correct answer and colour the pictures.

a. Animal science

b. Space science

c. Water science

d. Plant science

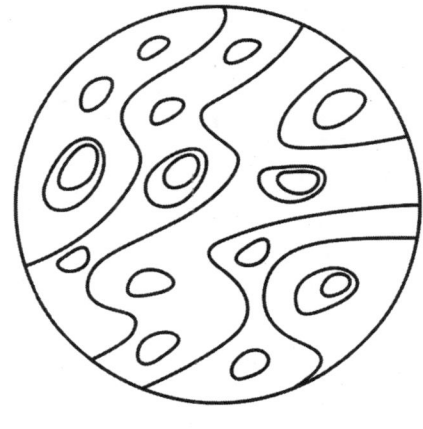
moon

star

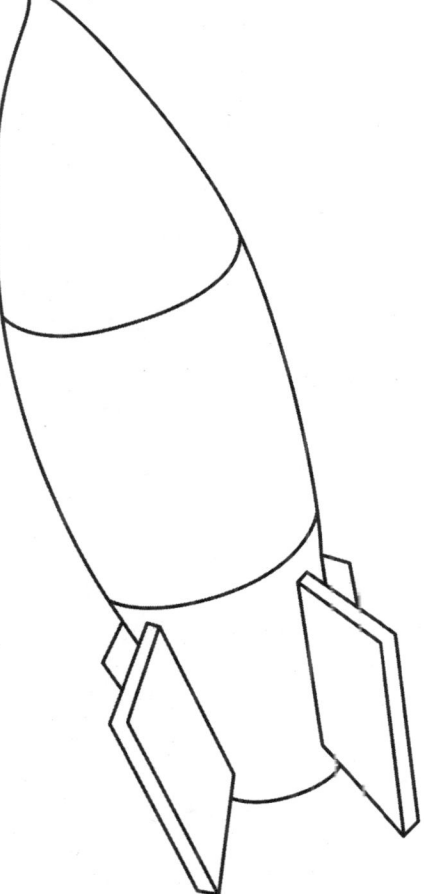
rocket

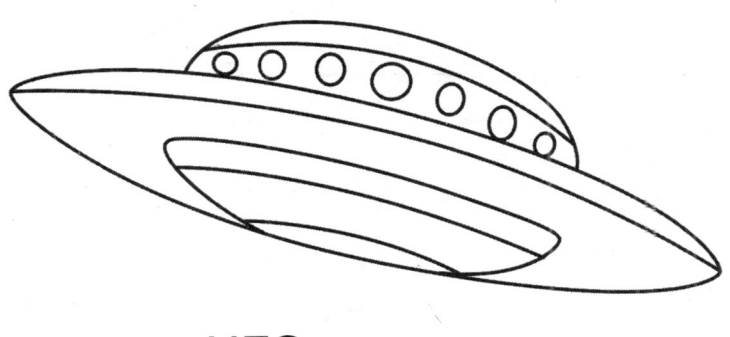
UFO

Date: _____ Teacher's Signature: _____

11 Rhyming Words

Choose the words from the Help Box that rhyme with the words given below.

Snack _____   Skin _____

That _____   Said _____

Pail _____   Toe _____

Froze _____   Fun _____

Groom _____   Split _____

Help Box

| Tale | Broom | Done | Grin | Sit | Bed | Glow |
| Nose | Flat | Black | | | | |

12 My Lunch Box

Colour those things that you can carry in a lunch box.

13 — My Favourite Storybook

Have you read storybooks? If yes, then this should be a simple activity for you.

Your favourite story: _____

Author of the book: _____

Favourite character from the book: _____

Draw the picture of your favourite character in this space.

Date: _____   Teacher's Signature: _____

14 Tool Tale

Look at the pictures in each box and answer.

Tick (✓) the tool used for cutting finger nails.

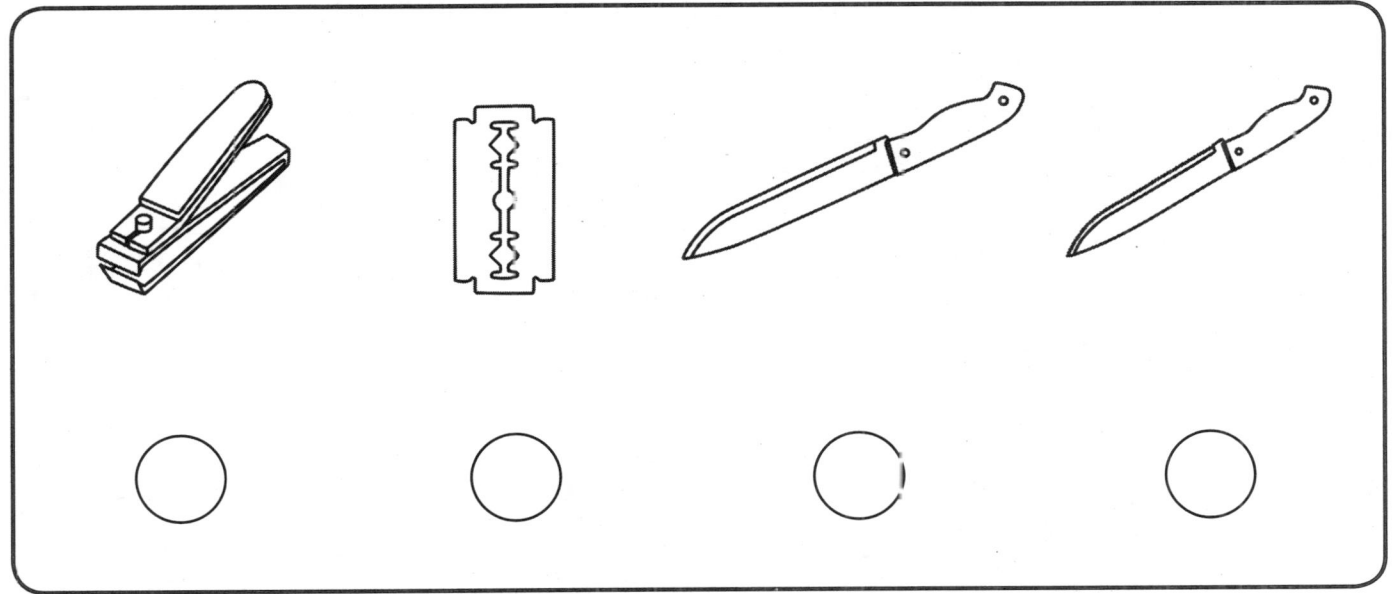

Tick mark (✓) the tool used for hitting nails.

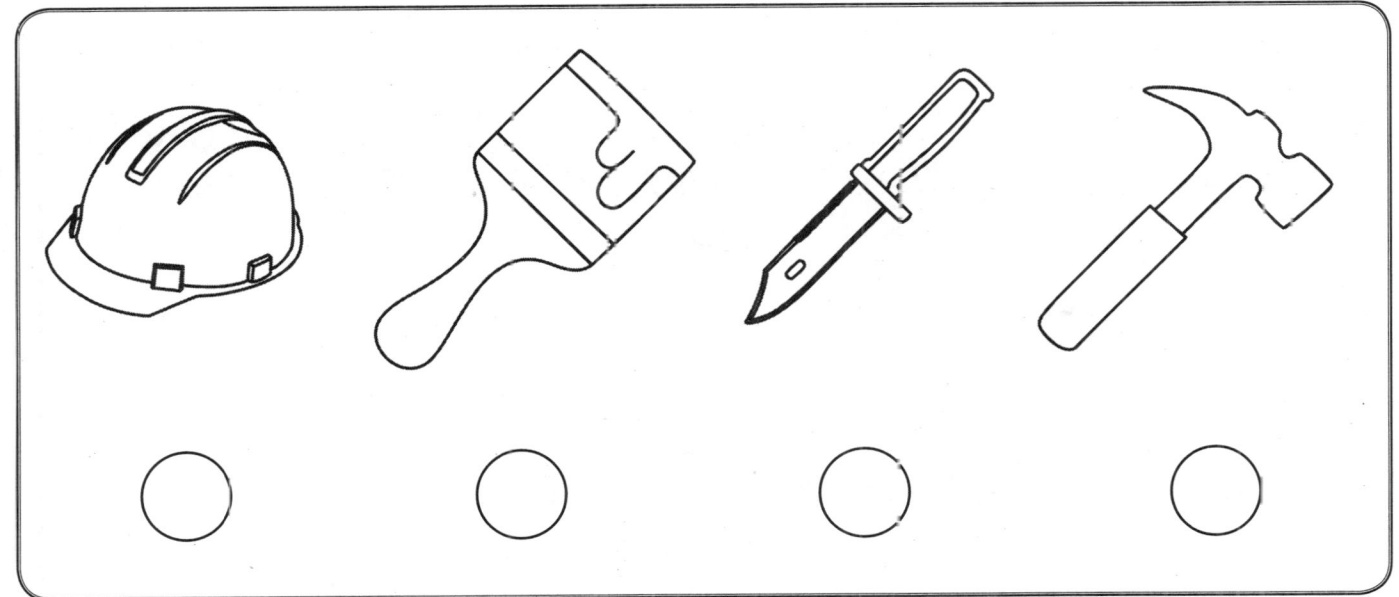

Date: _____ Teacher's Signature: _____

15 Mood Swings

Complete the sentences with the help of the emoticons.

Sam is so _____ because he is going on a vacation.

Diana is so _____ of dogs.

I feel so _____ after drinking milk at night.

When I am ____ , only my pet puppy can cheer me up.

When I am ____ , I like to play with my puppy.

Date: _____ Teacher's Signature: _____

16 A Weather Story

Describe the picture in three lines or in the form of a short story.

_____

_____

_____

Date: _____   Teacher's Signature: _____

17 Foodie Quiz

Identify the foods and answer the questions.

1. Which food should you eat for lunch?_____

2. Which of the food items is best for your health?_____

Date:_____   Teacher's Signature:_____

18 I Wish I Could Go To...

Complete the activity by filling the blank space, select a suitable option from the Help Box.

Help Box

mountains   beach   monuments   castles

My dream holiday place: _____

Draw and colour a picture of your dream holiday.

Date: _____   Teacher's Signature: _____

19 Where Are the Letters?

Fill in the missing letters to complete the words.

 __ __ ock

 __ __ wer

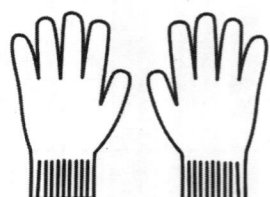 __ __ oves

 __ __ anket

 __ __ ue

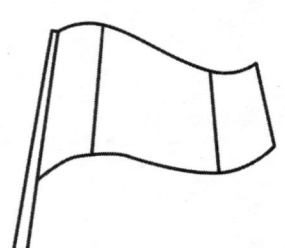 __ __ ag

 __ __ ips

 __ __ cks

Date: _____

Teacher's Signature: _____

20 Different Strokes

Look at the pictures and answer the questions.

Brush 1

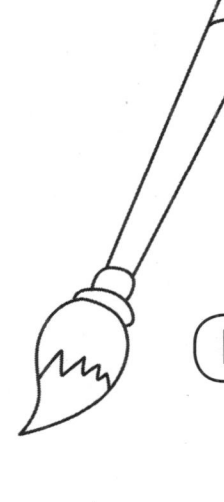
Brush 2

Brush 3

1. Which brush is used to paint the walls?_____

2. Which brush is suitable to paint a picture?_____

3. Which brush is used to clean your teeth? _____

Date: _____   Teacher's Signature: _____

21 Do I?

Look at the picture. Tick (✓) for 'yes' and (x) for 'no' for the questions accordingly.

Object	Do I need food and water?	Do I need air?	Do I grow?	Do I reproduce?	Am I living?
(chick)					
(fire)					
(clock)					
(ladybug)					

Date: _____   Teacher's Signature: _____

| 22 | **Natural or Artificial** |

Some pictures here are of things we find in nature and some are artificial or man made. Write 'N' for the things we find in nature and 'A' for man-made things.

23 Jack and Jill

Underline the words in the poem which are of things found in nature and circle all the artificial ones.

Jack and Jill went up the hill

To fetch a pail of water.

Jack fell down,

And broke his crown;

And Jill came tumbling after.

Then up Jack got, and home did trot,

as fast as he could caper.

They put him to bed, and plastered his head,

with vinegar and brown paper.

24 I Use My Nose To...

Write down the work the following body parts do for you.

I use my mouth to ___, ___ and ___.

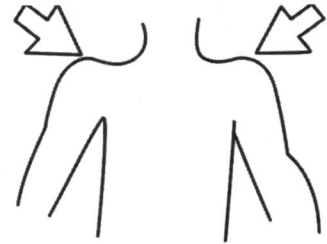
I use my shoulder to ___, ___ and ___.

I use my hands to ___, ___ and ___.

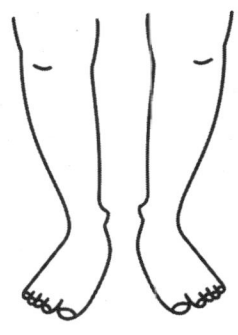
I use my legs to ___ and ___.

Date: _____   Teacher's Signature: _____

25 Yes and No!

While at home, you must follow certain rules. Write 'YES' below the thing you should or can do and 'NO' below tasks you should not or cannot do.

26 Judgement

Jack and his sister, Jessica, are at home. Their parents have gone out. Jack is six years old and his sister is three. Suddenly, Jessica falls down and cuts her knee. What should Jack do?

Tick (✓) in front of the correct option and make cross (x) for the wrong one.

1. He helps his sister up. ☐

2. He makes her sit comfortably on a chair. ☐

3. He pours cold water over the cut. ☐

4. He dabs some antiseptic on the wound with a cotton ball. ☐

5. He calls up his parents. ☐

6. He lets her cry till his parents come home. ☐

7. He keeps watching TV. ☐

Date: _____   Teacher's Signature: _____

27 Dog on Skateboard!

Colour the Picture.

28 Plant Search

Read the hints and unscramble the jumbled words to find out the names of these trees or plants.

This is a huge tree: **YNANAB** 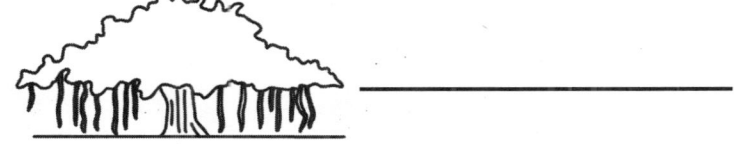 _____

This grows under the ground: **OTAOTP** 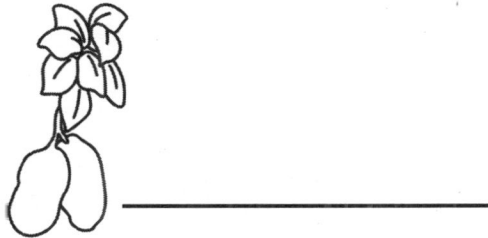 _____

This is a creeper: **MUCUCERB** 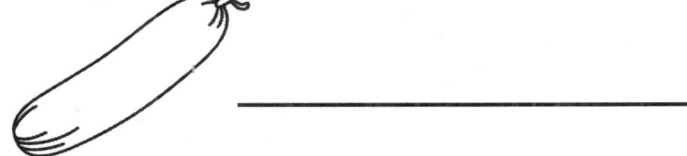 _____

This is a water plant: **ERATW LLYI** 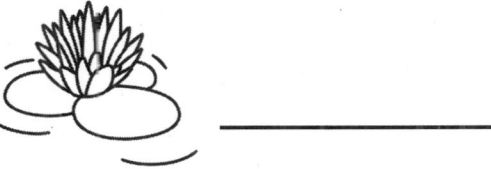 _____

This grows on hills: **ENPI** 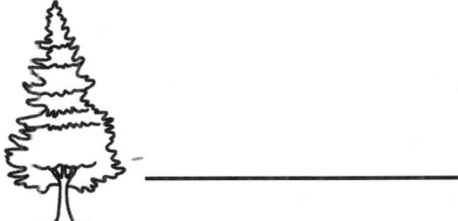 _____

Date: _____   Teacher's Signature: _____

29 | The Missing Ones

Which part or parts are missing from the tree here? Draw the missing parts.

Date: _____

Teacher's Signature: _____

30 Who Am I? Where Do I Live?

Identify these animals and write 'C' for companion or pet animals or 'W' for wild in front of them. Match them with the place they live in.

Forest   Home/neighbourhood

31 Picture Heading

Look at the picture. Give a heading that describes the picture.

32 Animal Name Puzzle

Find the names of the animals in the alphabet grid with the help of the hints given below.

Who am I?

(a) I have four legs but I crawl on the ground.

(b) I can swim in water.

(c) I have a shell to hide.

L	T	C	L	A	F	I	X
Y	I	T	V	X	I	K	O
M	A	N	T	O	S	Z	X
A	H	Z	U	G	H	T	Y
E	Z	F	R	M	U	G	V
A	J	Y	T	H	A	M	W
Z	K	E	L	Z	J	G	V
H	Z	Z	E	R	D	S	Z

Date: _____   Teacher's Signature: _____

33 In the Sky

Circle the words in the box that are related to these pictures.

| AIR | WATER | HEAVY | FLY | LIGHT | WINGS |
| STRING | TAIL | | | | |

Tasty Eggs

1. Which egg preparation is the tastiest?

Rank from 1-3:

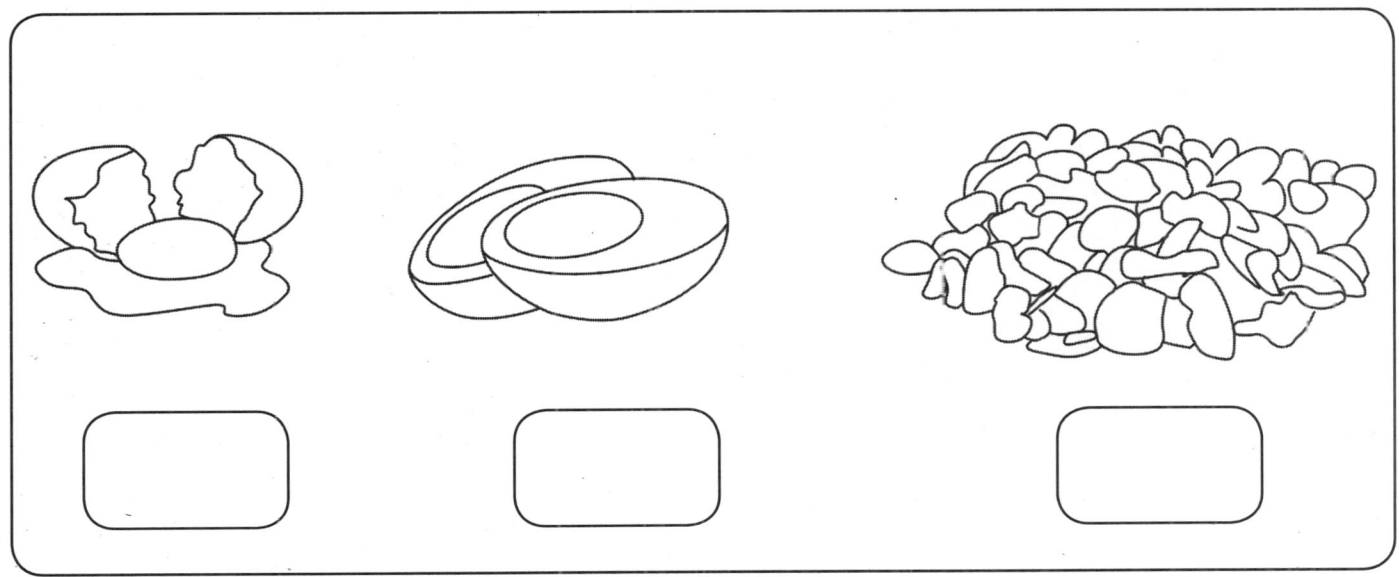

2. Which is the raw form? Tick (✓) the correct answer.

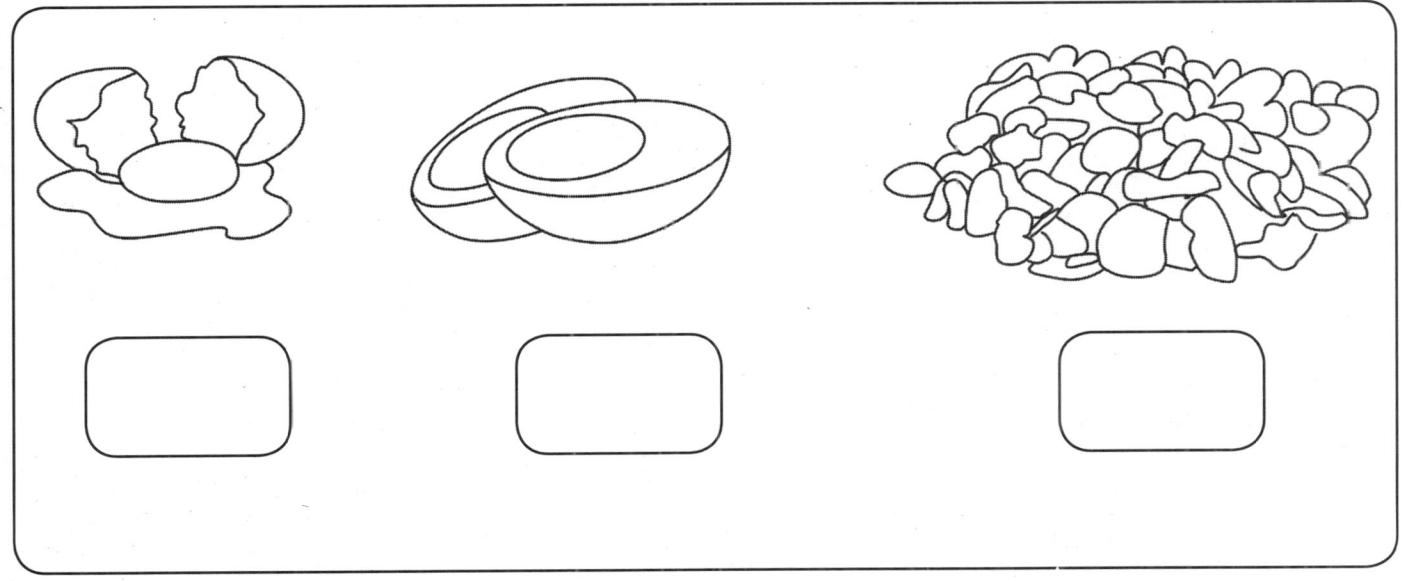

Date: _____ Teacher's Signature: _____

35 Healthy vs Junk

 Junk Sugar-Rich Food

 Junk Oily Food

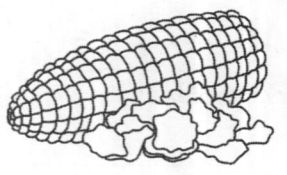 Healthy Drink

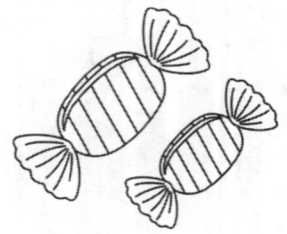 Healthy Snack

 Healthy Sugar-Rich Food

Date: _____   Teacher's Signature: _____

36 Running Sam

Complete the story of Sam with the help of words in the Help Box.

Help Box

| man | fan | van | can | ran |

This _____'s name is Sam.

He _____ run very fast.

He has a big _____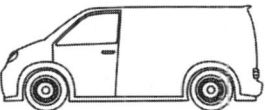

and a beautiful _____.

One day, his _____  was stolen and then he lost his ____

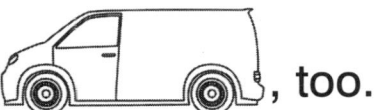, too.

So, he _____ all around the town to look for them.

Date: _____   Teacher's Signature: _____

37 Chew, Chew and Chew!

Circle and Colour the foods that need lots of chewing.

   Corn Cob

   Cake

   Pineapple

   Apple pie

Date: _____   Teacher's Signature: _____

38 Witty Tagline

Look at the following pictures and give each one a witty tagline.

39 Building Blocks

Find the words given in the box from the alphabet grid.

Help Box

1. BRICK
2. TILES
3. CEMENT
4. IRON
5. SAND
6. WOOD
7. STRAW
8. BAMBOO

Q	T	C	S	A	N	D
Y	T	E	Y	B	W	Z
B	I	M	S	A	O	I
R	L	E	T	M	O	R
I	E	N	R	B	D	O
C	S	T	A	O	A	N
K	K	L	W	O	E	Q

What are these materials used for? _____

Date: _____   Teacher's Signature: _____

40 Clean My House

Identify the things in the picture and find out how they help in cleaning the house?

_____

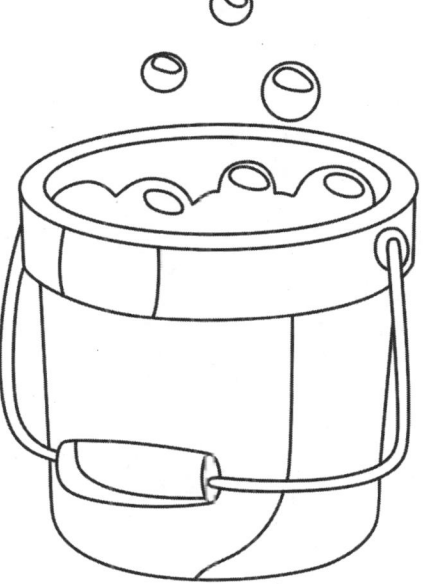
_____

_____

_____

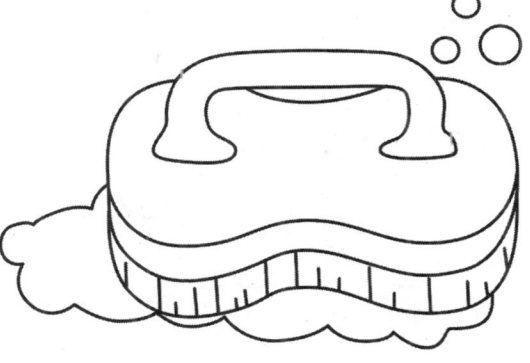
_____

Date: _____   Teacher's Signature: _____

47 Picture Message

What messages do these pictures convey? Give each one an interesting title.

42   Spic and Span

Inspect various places in your neighbourhood (park, playground, home, yard, school, etc.) and grade them. The grade system is given below:

5 – Excellent cleanliness

4 – Good cleanliness

3 – Average cleanliness

2 – Poor cleanliness

1 – Very bad

Place	Cleanliness Grade	Remark

Date: _____   Teacher's Signature: _____

43 Waste Matters

Match the following.

a.  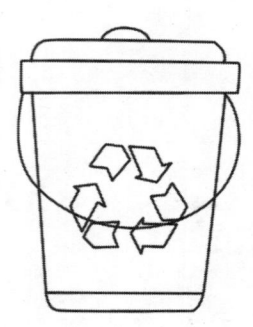   1. Roadside bins

b. 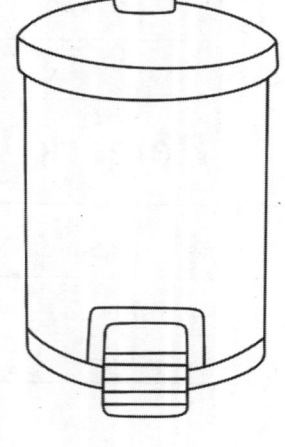   2. Green waste bins

c. 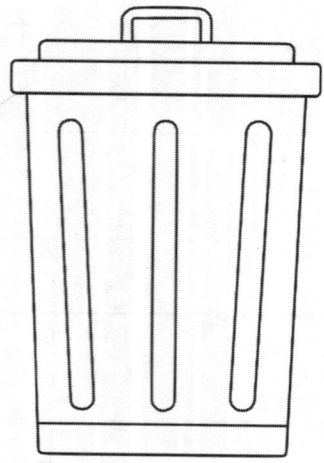   3. Household dustbins

This Flower's Odd

Do you think all the flowers are same? Look at the picture and circle the odd one out.

45 Pat on the Back

Put a tick (✓) on the pictures of children who will get a pat on their back.

Make a Rhyme Chain

Read the words and complete the rhyming word chain.

Rain → Drain → _____

Meal → Feel → _____

Mob → Rob → _____

Deep → Sleep → _____

Clip → Slip → _____

Date: _____   Teacher's Signature: _____

My Role Model

What do you want to become when you grow up? Look at the pictures given below and circle the picture that inspires you.

48 Refrigerate Me

Look the pictures given below. Write their names and circle the things that are kept in a refrigerator.

Work We Do

Match each picture with the sentence that describes the work they do.

I deliver letters

I rescue people from drowning

I cook food in a restaurant

I paint walls

I put out fire and help people in emergency

Date: _____

Teacher's Signature: _____

50 Who Will Eat Whom?

Number the pictures given below as 1, 2, 3, 4 in order of who eats whom. The first one has been done for you.

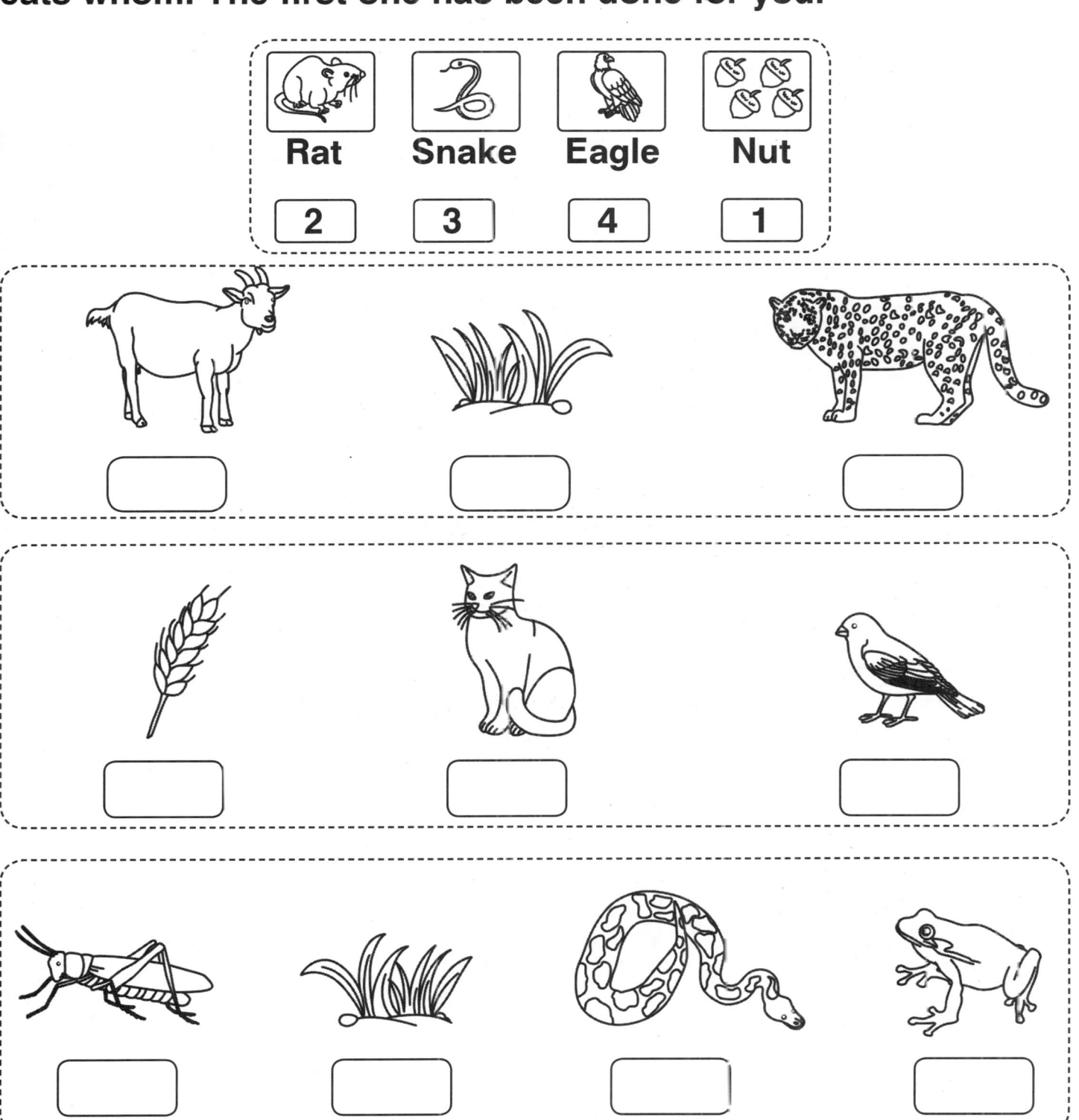

51 Find My Home

Circle the pictures that are homes to animals or human beings.

Fish

Apple

Kennel

Goat

Home

Cake

Barn

Jar

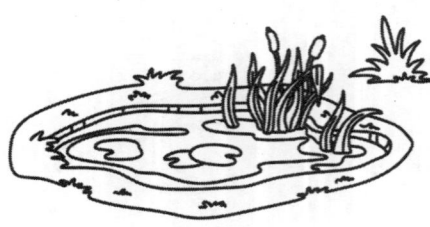
Pond

Hat

Den

Date: _____   Teacher's Signature: _____

52 Knowing Colours!

Lucas visited a garden and saw the following flowers and vegetables. Can you tell the colours of those flowers and vegetables?

53 Find the Verb

Verbs are words used to describe an action. Now, complete the sentences using the verbs given in the Help Box.

Help Box

gives	has	starts	think
know	asks	slices	walks

1. Jammy _____ many pets.

2. Martin _____ running at 6 am.

3. Nanny ____ the apple into four pieces to make an apple pie.

4. I don't _____ at what time he would come today.

5. Mr. Anderson _____ me for change.

6. Lucy _____ a mile to school.

7. I _____ about my dream the previous night.

8. Simmy _____ Tina her evening snack.

Helping Hands

Look at the animals below. What do they give us?

..............................Egg/Wool/Milk

..............................Egg/Wool/Milk

..............................Egg/Wool/Milk

Date: _____   Teacher's Signature: _____

55 People and Places

Name of a person, place, animal or thing is called noun. Write the naming words from the Help Box in the correct category.

Help Box

| Store | Zoo | Child | Baby | Table | Cat | Mother |
| Woman | Watch | Glass | Horse | Park | Forest | |

Person — Teacher

Animal — Rabbit

Place — School

Thing — Clock

56 Find the Adjective

Adjectives are words that describe a noun. Match the nouns with suitable adjectives.

   Puppy   Little

   Weather   Sticky

   Ant   Wet

   Hair   Cute

   Glue   Hot

57 Nouns and Verbs

Identify the nouns and verbs in the following sentences and write them down in the correct column.

	Noun	Verb
The sun shines.		
The wind blows.		
The flowers bloom.		
The dog barks.		
The fish swims.		
The leaf falls.		
The moon shines.		

Date: _____   Teacher's Signature: _____

58 Seasonal Fruits

Write the names of three fruits that are associated with the four seasons given here. You can take the help of an elders.

Seasons	Fruits
Summer	
Rain	
Winter	
Spring	

Date: _____   Teacher's Signature: _____

Carrot Dish

1. Which preparation of carrot is the tastiest? Rank from 1-3.

2. Which is the raw form? Tick (✓) the correct answer.

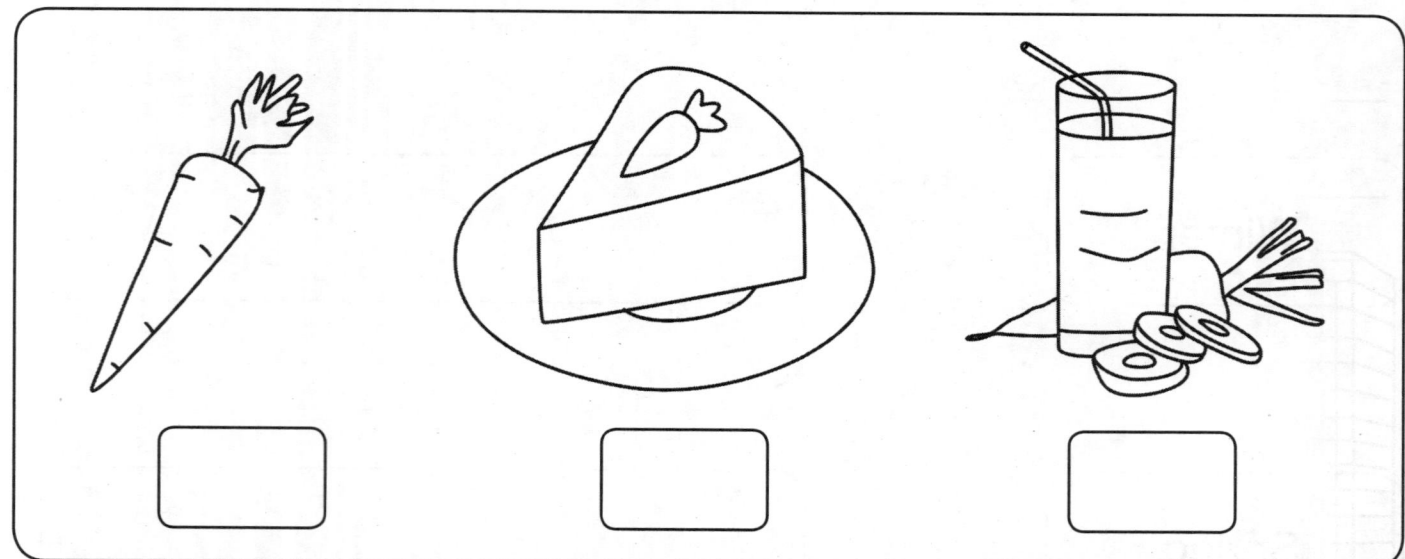

60 What is that?

Identify the pictures and describe one feature about each in one sentence.

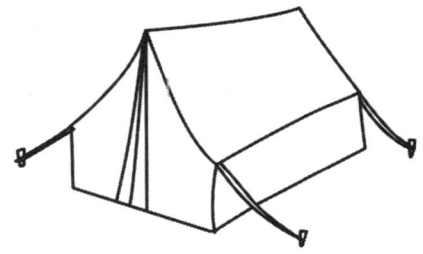

_____

_____

_____

_____

_____

_____

_____

_____

_____

_____

Date: _____   Teacher's Signature: _____

Spell Out

61

Identify these simple, everyday things and spell them out.

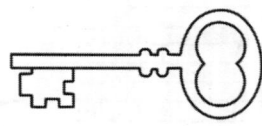 _____

 _____

 _____

 _____

 _____

 _____

Date: _____   Teacher's Signature: _____

62 Singular and Plural

Identify the things that are singular and those that are plural. One has been done for you.

Singular	Plural
Key	Pencils

Date: _____   Teacher's Signature: _____

Punctuation Match

Identify the punctuation and match.

Question mark !

Full stop

?

Exclamation mark ,

Comma .

64 Question or Full Stop?

Read the sentences and put the correct punctuation marks, full stop (.) or question mark (?), at the end of each sentence.

I love apples

Do you eat apple

What is the colour of a carrot

The flowers smell very nice

Do you see the worms

It's a nice sunny day today

Date: _____   Teacher's Signature: _____

We are Opposites

Draw a line and match the opposites.

Slow	Back
Full	Outside
Front	Wild animals
Inside	Sour
Sweet	Empty
Pets	Fast

Date: _____

Teacher's Signature: _____

Julia's Letter

Julia wants to write a letter to her friend. Help her complete the letter by putting correct punctuation marks.

Hi __ How are you __ I am at a camp __ I am having a great time here __ There are so many activities to do here every day __ I love horse riding __ playing volleyball and sitting around with everyone near the camp fire at night __ How are your holidays going __ I will see you after the holidays __

Your friend
   Julia

67 Rescuing Annie!

Help the Annie the ant, find her way through the castle. There is an anteater on the way, make sure that Annie avoids him.

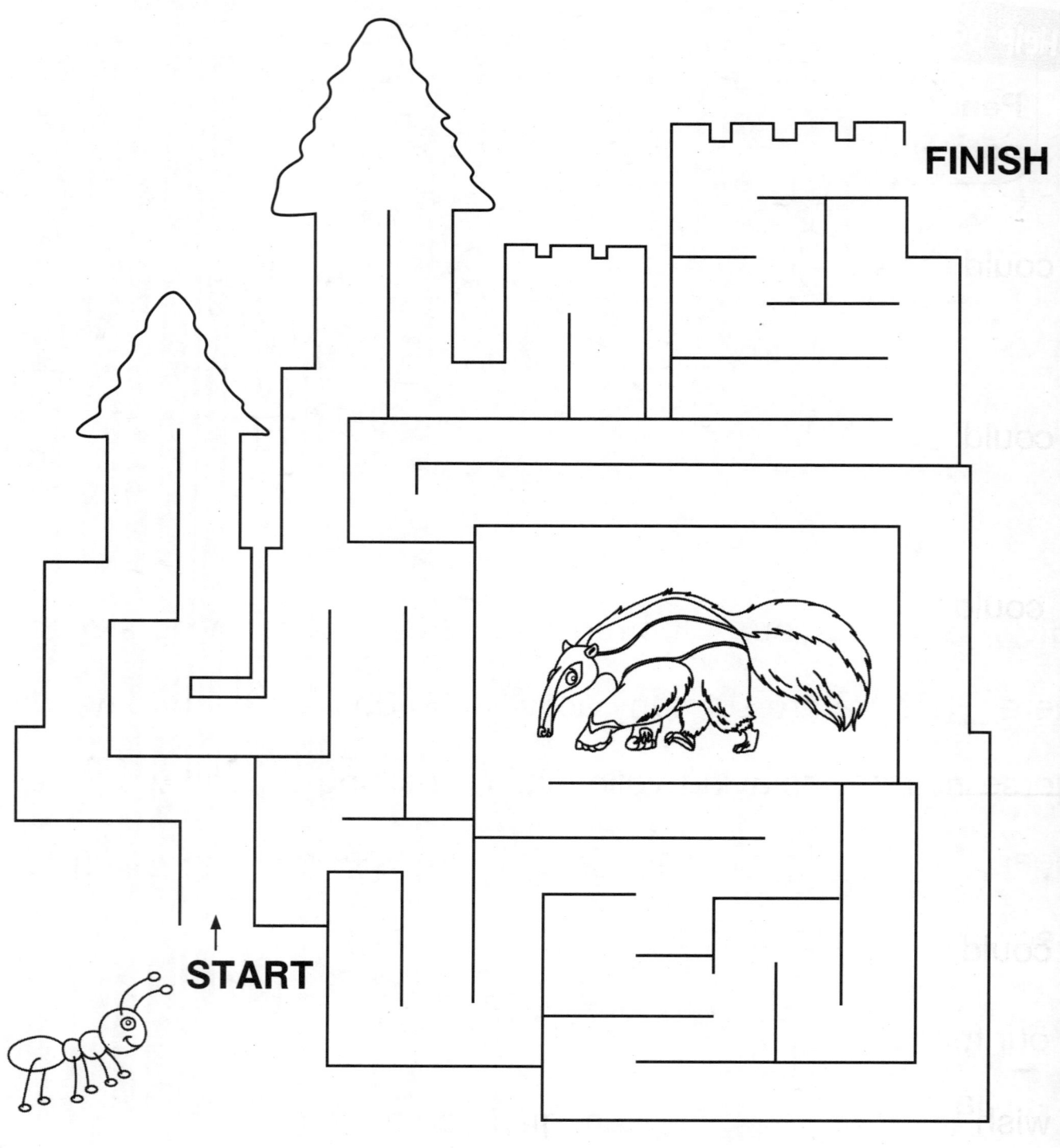

50-50

Fill in the blanks with appropriate pair of words from the Help Box.

Help Box

| Pencils | books | feet | miles | chips |
| potatoes | toothpicks | plates | toys | chores |

I could carry 50 ____, but I couldn't carry 50 _____.

I could eat 50 ___, but I couldn't eat 50 _____.

I could put 50 _____ in my backpack, but I couldn't put 50 _____ in my backpacks.

I could walk 50 ___, but I couldn't walk 50 ___!

I wish I had 50 ____, but I am glad I do not have to do 50 _____.

Date: _____   Teacher's Signature: _____

69 Sentence From a Box

Identify the things in the picture and use the words in the box to form a sentence. You can also colour the picture.

Help Box

| Flowers | colours | are | many | of |

Sentence: _____

_____

Date: _____   Teacher's Signature: _____

10 Know Your Body

Use the names of various parts of the body in the Help Box to label the picture.

Help Box

Toes Hair Knee Arms Hand Legs Lips
Cheeks Ears Elbow

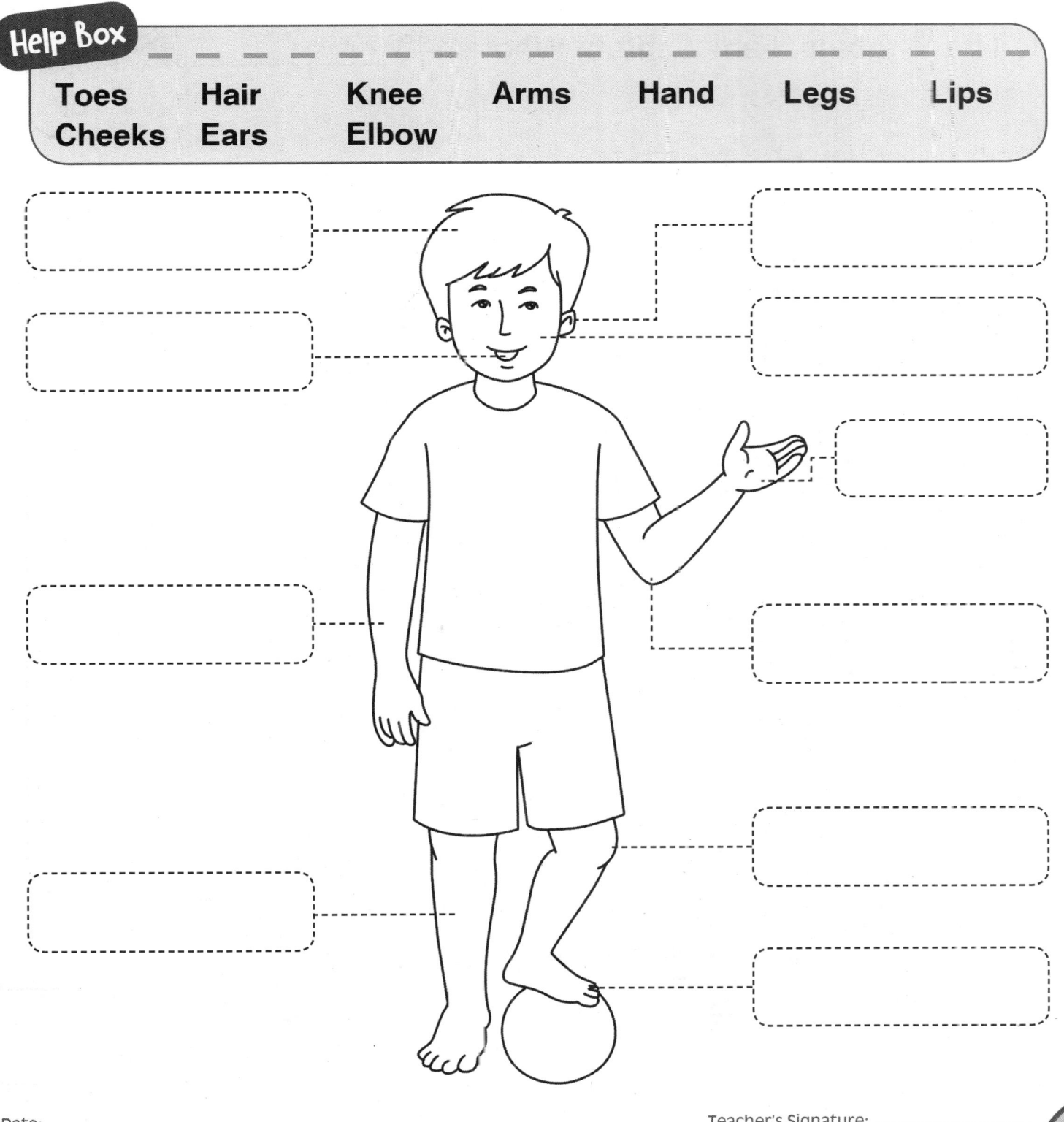

71 Who Am I?

Identify these things based on the clues.

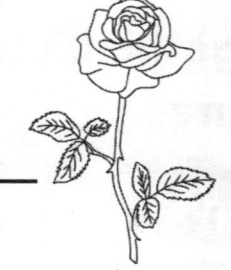

1. I have thorns. I am a shrub. Who am I? _____

2. I grow on a very tall tree. I am a round fruit. If I fall on someone's head, he may faint. Which fruit am I? _____

3. I am a vegetable plant. I have a weak stem. The colour of my vegetable is purple, green, or white. Who am I? _____

4. Fruits of my plant are sweet. I am a tall plant with very thick stem. My fruits come in summer. Who am I? _____

Date: _____   Teacher's Signature: _____

72 Winter World

Fill in the correct letters and complete the names of various things related to the winters. Then, match the words with the pictures.

Help Box

gl   cl   pi   wi   sn   sc

__ __ owman

__ __ ne

__ __ oves

__ __ arf

__ __ nd

__ __ oud

73 Hungry Billy and the Grass

Little Billy the goat is very hungry. Please help him get to the grass.

My Hairstyle

Complete the faces and colour the hair.

75 Where Are We?

Can you recognise the place in the picture? Read the clues to find out and then fill in the blanks.

Clue Box
1. This place has snow everywhere.
2. We can see beautiful penguin families here.

This is a _____ (snow-clad mountain/desert region)

I would love to _____ (ski/swim) here.

Date: _____   Teacher's Signature: _____

76 I Am Crawling

Look at the picture and use the words in the box to form two sentences.

_____

_____

_____

77 Wordsmith

Make a new word by changing the first letter of each word with a new letter from the box. Circle the correct answer.

	RUN	M N S	
	DOLL	T R O	
	BREAD	T H Z	
	LOG	D R W	
	EAR	G M C	

Date: _____   Teacher's Signature: _____

My Time to Write!!

1. My favourite food is _____

2. My favourite animal is _____

3. I live at home with _____

   _____

4. My favourite room at home is _____

   _____

5. The country where I live is _____

6. The state where live is _____

   _____

79 Find Word, Make Sentence

Search the words from the word block and form a sentence.

_____

_____

_____

H	Z	C	X	Q
A	G	T	I	T
P	I	D	S	H
P	R	R	C	E
Y	L	B	K	O

Date: _____ Teacher's Signature: _____

Sporty Tale

Identify the sport and find and write the name of one famous player who is associated with this game.

Name of the sport: _____

Famous Player: _____

Date: _____ Teacher's Signature: _____

81 The Lost Alphabet

Complete the word by filling in the missing alphabet at the end.

Cro__

Gir__

Berr__

Nes__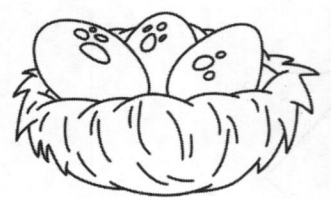

Curl__

Two Missing Alphabets

Fill in the two missing alphabets and complete the given words.

> **Clue Box**
> The missing alphabets are common to all the words.

r _ _ n   tr _ _ n   p _ _ nt

m _ _ l n   _ _ l n   st _ _ n

83 Who Am I?

Identify the creature in the picture and colour it. You can also give it a cute name. _____

84 Happy Girl

Use the words in the Help Box to make two meaningful sentences based on the picture.

Help Box

jumps   happy   girl   the   is   up   high

85 What Is It?

What is happening in the picture here? How will you define this?

Picture Brief

Observe the picture carefully and write what is happening between the two characters.

_____

_____

_____

Date: _____   Teacher's Signature: _____

Where Do We Belong?

Which of the animals here are found in the jungle? Colour them.

88 It's Father's Day!

Use your father's favourite colours to colour the picture. Write one line about your father in the circle.

89 Simple Crossword

Complete the crossword with the help of the hints.

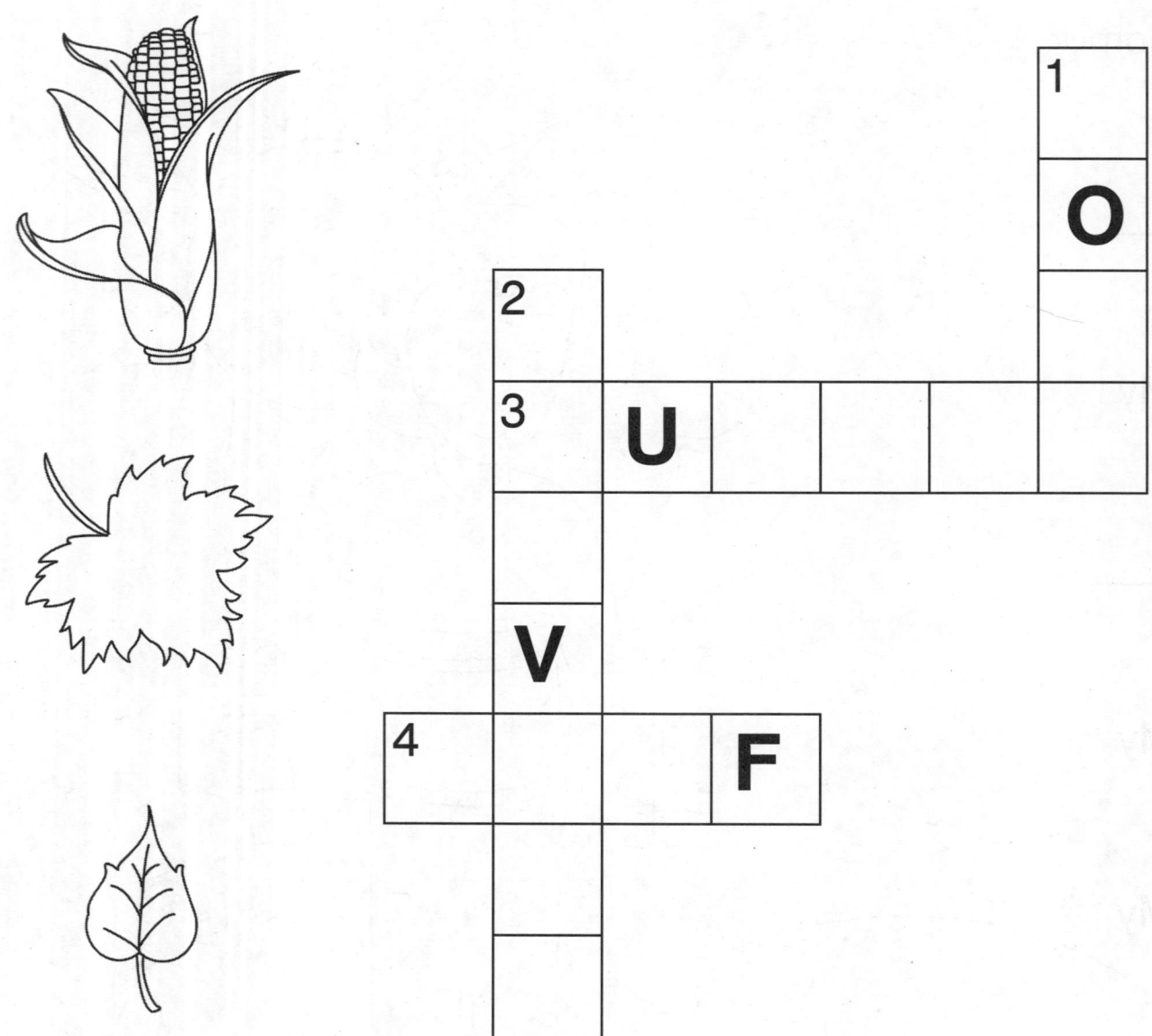

Across:
3. The season when leaves fall from the trees.
4. Green part of a plant or tree

Down
1. A vegetable which has seeds as an edible part of it.
2. Process of collecting foods that have been grown.

90 Writer's Box

Complete the following sequences by filling the blanks.

1. Some of my friends are named _____

   _____

2. My favourite sport is _____ because _____

   _____

3. My favourite kind of music is _____

4. My favourite song is _____

5. My favourite subject in school is _____

6. My favourite teacher's name is _____

Date: _____   Teacher's Signature: _____

97 Parts of a Lily

Label the lily plant with the help of hints in the Help Box.

Help Box

Petal	Stem	Root	Leaf

Date: ____________ Teacher's Signature: ____________

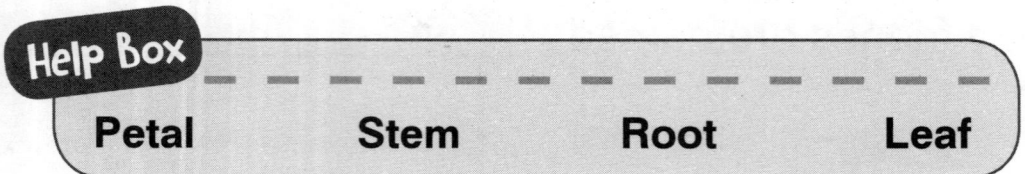

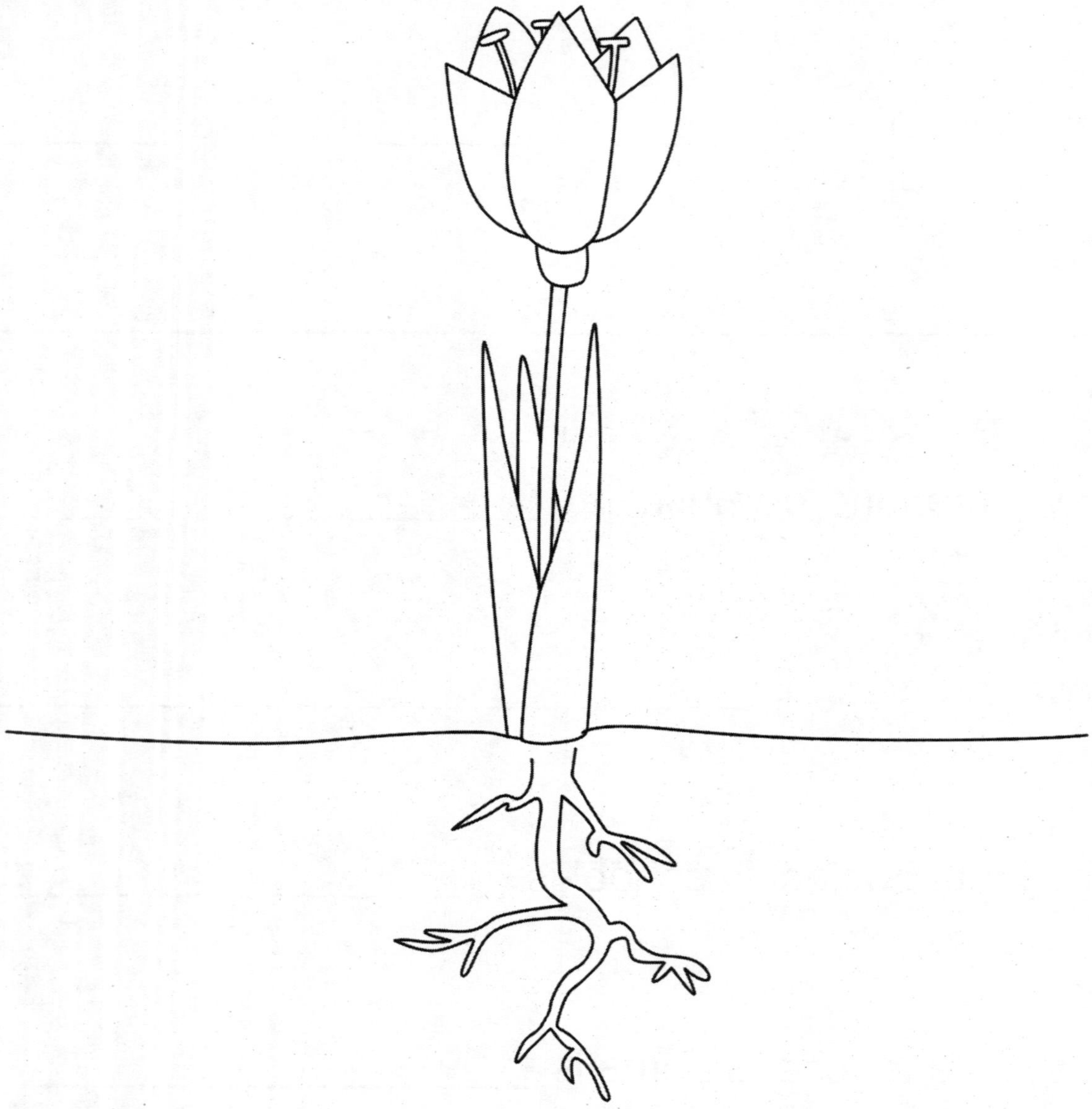

Past Link

Match things from the past and present according to their use.

93 Riding a Horse

Colour the picture and give a name to both the characters in the picture. Use your imagination to give the picture a suitable title

Title: _____

94 — Me, My House and the Tree

My house is red – a little house;
A happy child am I.
I laugh and play the whole day long,
I hardly ever cry.

I have a tree, a green, green tree,
To shade me from the sun;
And under it I often sit,
When all my play is done.

Colour the picture given above according to the poem.

1. What is the colour of the house that the child lives in?_____

2. When does the child sit under the tree?_____

95 It's Time for Puzzle

Fill in the blanks using the letters given at the end of each clue.

Often produced by vehicles and dirt the air: O, P, L, I, N

__ __ L __ UT __ O __

Cars, Trucks, Ships, Bus, Airplanes are all forms of this: T, P, N, S, R

TRA __ __ __ O __ __

Mercury, Venus, Earth and Jupiter are examples of this: T, P, E, S

__ LAN __ __ __

Water Bodies

Circle the pictures of animals that live in water.

97 Hug for a Friend

Colour the picture first. Remember the time when you gave your friend a hug. Write two such instances here.

1. _____
2. _____

Date: _____   Teacher's Signature: _____

Word Search

Search the words in the given word maze.

P	N	C	U	T	E	E	M	U	E	X	O
D	U	E	F	M	B	C	U	W	O	M	H
K	B	L	U	E	K	W	L	O	L	C	Z
P	T	F	L	G	L	U	E	J	V	L	D
T	U	B	E	Q	U	J	N	B	V	S	K
M	U	L	P	X	Y	U	R	U	L	E	T
U	I	H	G	G	Z	I	C	P	K	A	X
T	Y	O	I	N	T	C	U	U	C	A	P
E	D	M	A	E	U	E	B	K	Y	O	U
R	S	B	I	R	N	J	E	Z	Y	I	I
L	R	C	Z	U	S	E	G	W	U	K	P
Z	O	S	Y	C	O	Y	V	B	C	C	F

CUBE	RULE	CUTE	MUTE
TUBE	MULE	USE	YOU
GLUE	DUE	JUICE	BLUE

99 Their Lunch

Look at the animal pictures here. What will they eat for lunch? Give your answers in the given space.

100 The Right Pair

Choose the correct pair of letters to complete the words. Then match the words with the suitable picture.

Help Box

dr   st   st   pl   it   fr

__ __ ess

__ __ ar

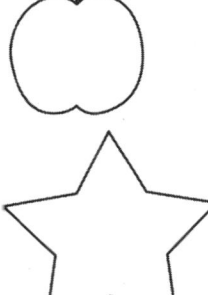

Toa __ __

__ __ anet

Fru __ __

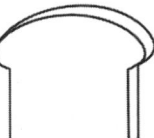

__ __ ont

101 Finish My Sentence

Adjectives are words that describe a noun. Complete the sentences with some adjectives.

For example: I had a very tasty lunch today.

1. Today I feel _____.

2. I decided to wear a _____ shirt.

3. My lunch was _____.

4. I am wearing a _____ watch today.

5. I had a _____ walk to the market today.

6. I saw a _____ lion in the zoo.

7. The _____ flower in my garden blooms every day.

8. My _____ friends played in the park.

Date: _____   Teacher's Signature: _____

Capital Task

Rule no. 1: Start the sentence with a capital letter.
Rule no. 2: Start names of people/place/animals or things with capital letter.

Now use these rules and correct the following sentences:

1. my dog max can fetch me a ball from the ground.

   _____

   _____

2. the christmas party is on friday.

   _____

   _____

3. mom, when can I go to play outside?

   _____

   _____

Date: _____   Teacher's Signature: _____

103 Sentence Puzzle

Get clues from the next sentence to complete the one before it.

I have a pet. It is a _____.

My pet cat is of _____ colour.

I named my black cat Roxy. She plays with me in the _____ every evening.

Last evening, she caught a rat in the park.

104 Now and Then

Write 'Past' in front of the things people did or used in the past and write 'Present' for activities people do or things they use in today's world.

1. We watch TV. _____

2. We use telegram. _____

3. We use computer. _____

4. We travel by a horse cart. _____

5. We use fire wood to cook food. _____

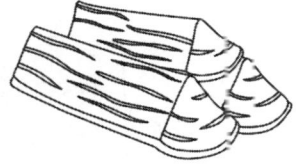

6. We use mobile phone to make calls. _____

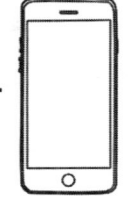

Date: _____ Teacher's Signature: _____

105 Things or Work

Look at the pictures given below. Write 'T' for things and 'A' for action.

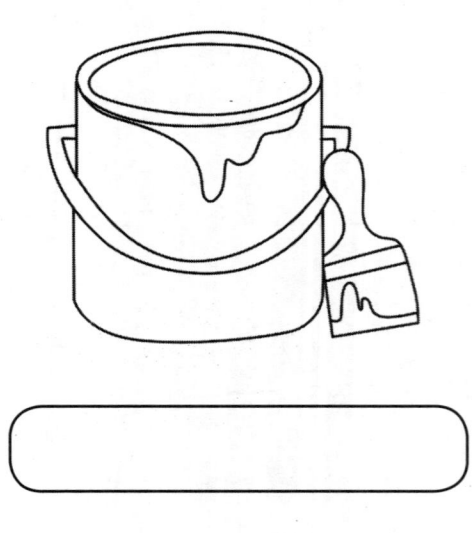

106 On the Job

Match the profession with the type of tool they use.

Traffic Policeman

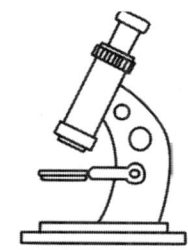

Chef

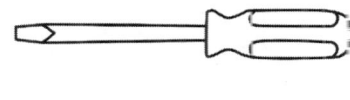

Scientist

Mechanic

Farmer

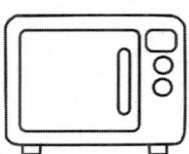

107 I Am...

Match the pictures with a suitable word that describes it.

 Salty

 Big

 Soft

 Sharp

 Sweet

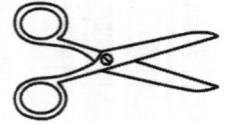 Loud

My Healthy Diet Chart

Fill in the table with a healthy food of your choice.

Food Type	Your Choice
Plant root/stem	
Plant leaf	
Plant seed	
Plant fruit/vegetable	
Animal product	
Animal product	

Date: _____

Teacher's Signature: _____

109 Noun's Cousin

He, She, It, They, My, Mine are pronouns. They can be used in place of noun. Now, use the correct pronoun with the following pictures.

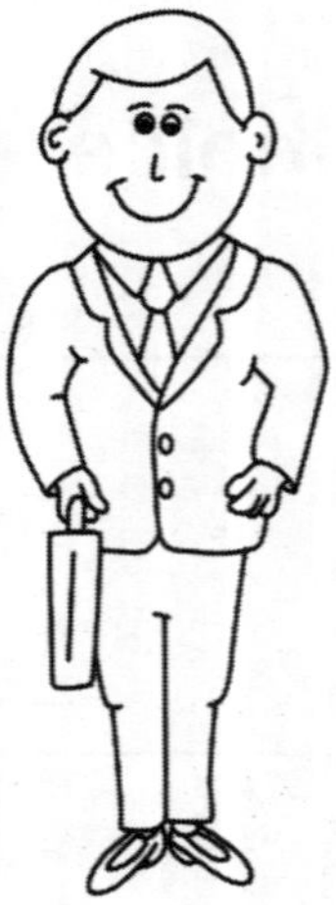

He

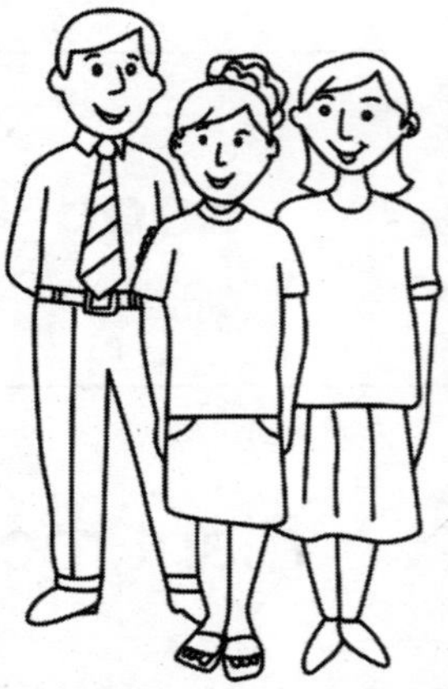

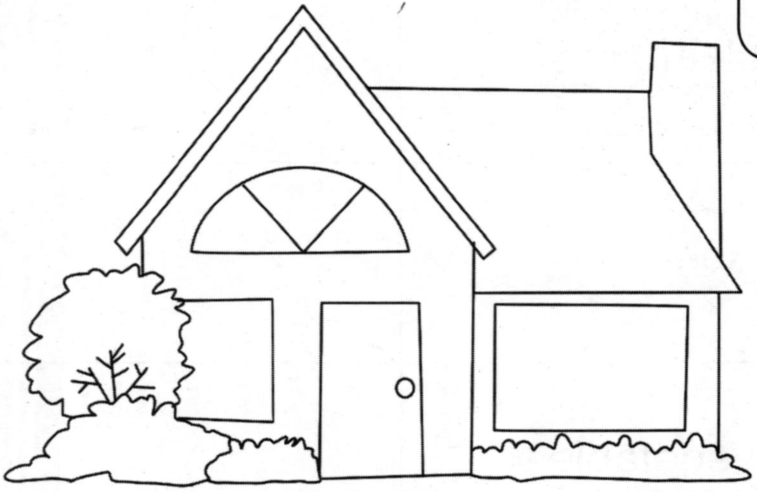

This is ________ house. (mine/my).

Date: ________ Teacher's Signature: ________

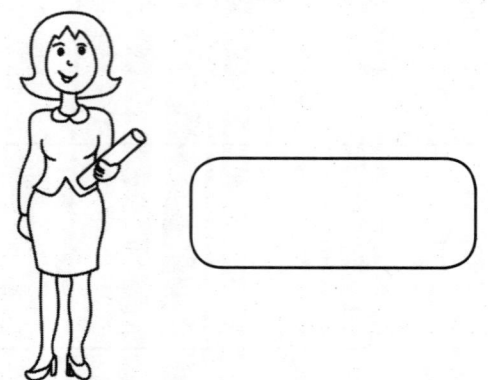

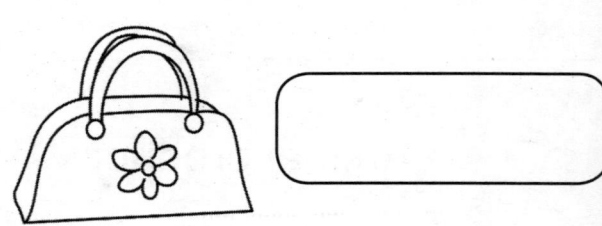

Reuse, Recycle, Reduce

Discuss with your parents and write one word for each of them: 'Reuse', 'Recycle', or 'Reduce'

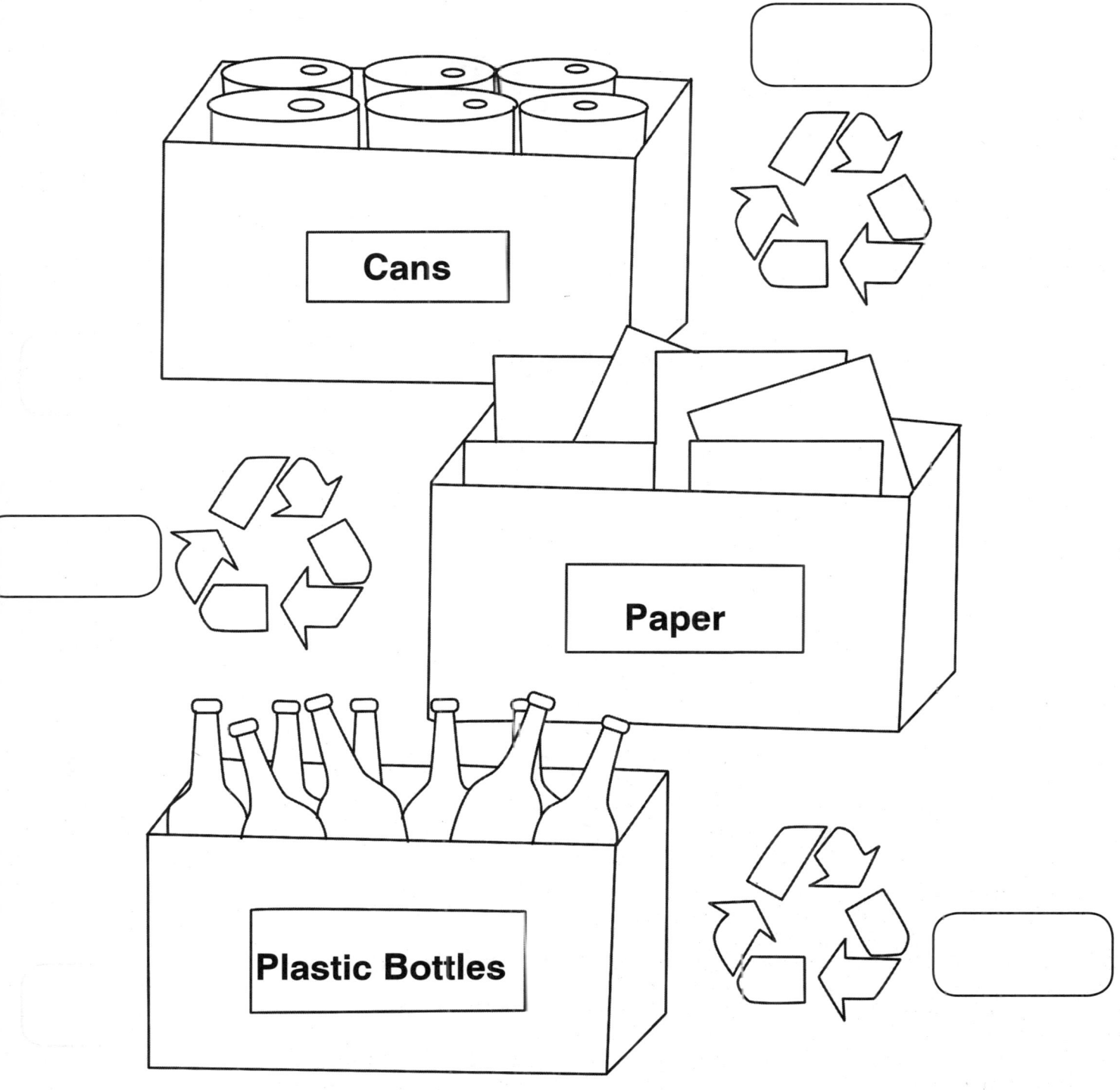

111 Easter Word Hunt

Search for these Easter-related words in the alphabet grid.

Help Box

| Easter | Hunt | Spring | Egg | Bunny | Tulip |

L	B	U	N	N	Y	S	W	O
E	G	G	D	G	W	P	A	A
J	V	Q	D	Q	I	R	F	B
L	J	N	H	A	S	I	T	R
N	X	W	V	L	E	N	A	U
I	C	E	T	A	A	G	H	S
H	T	Q	U	G	S	Z	U	P
Y	T	U	L	A	T	U	N	H
R	X	Z	I	R	E	P	T	U
A	A	Z	P	G	R	C	E	N

Date: _____

Teacher's Signature: _____

112 Different Surroundings

Look at the two pictures in each box. Can you see the differences? Write any two differences in the blank spaces.

1

2

1. _____

2. _____

Date: _____   Teacher's Signature: _____

113 Rhyming Crossword

Solve the crossword with the help of hints. Each answer rhymes with a word in the Help Box.

Help Box

| Grate | Trip | Proud | Price |
| Grass | Trash | Train | Grain |

Down: 1. Drain, 2. Loud, 4. Class

Across: 1. Slip, 2. Chain, 3. Crash, 4. Slate

114 Water! Water!

Choose the correct words for both the categories and fill in the blanks.

Help Box

| Rivers | Underground water | Drinking | Bathing |
| Ponds | Rain | Washing | |

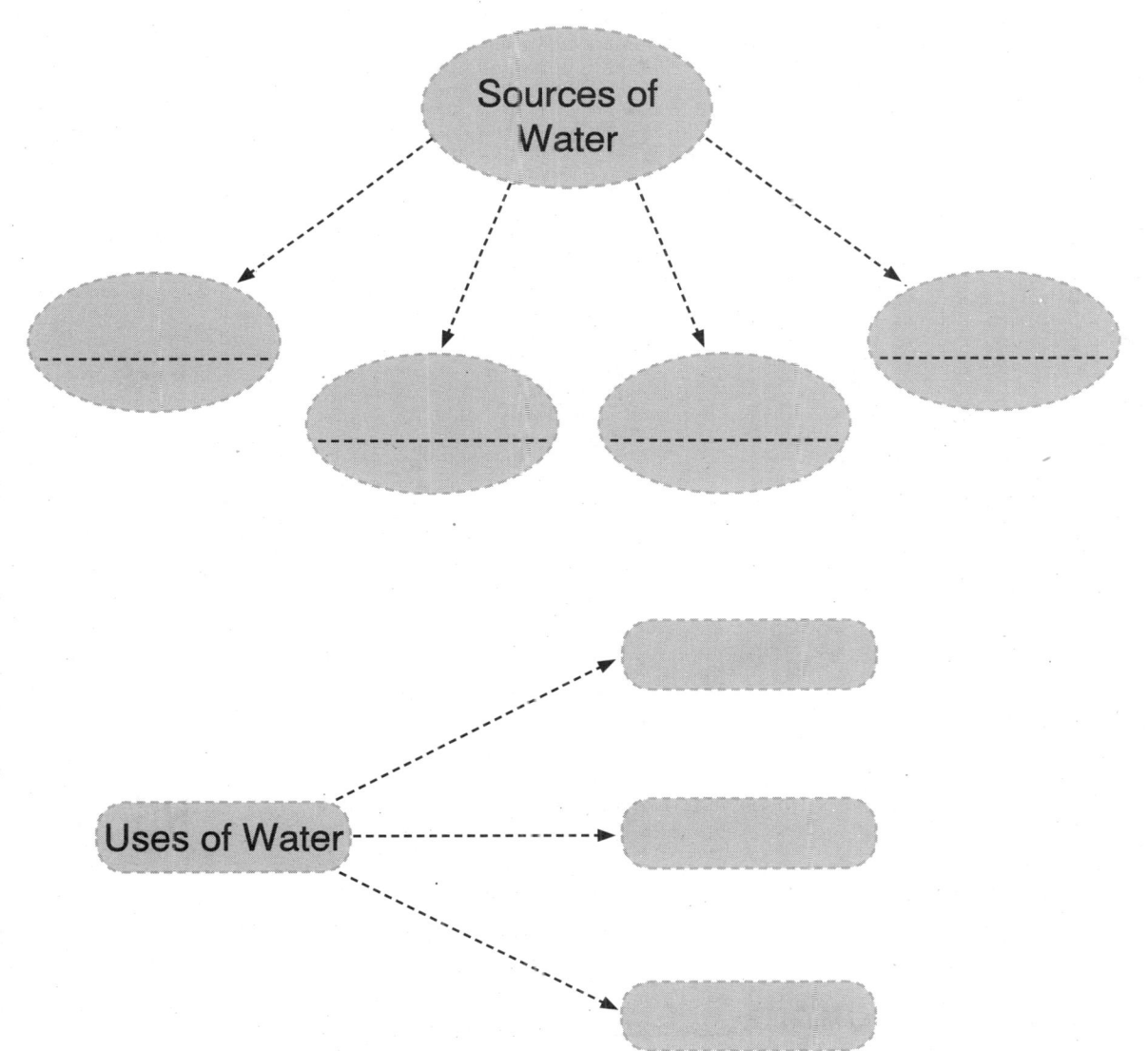

115 Three-Step Task

Read the words and complete the task in three steps.

Step 1: Read the words

Step 2: Circle the nouns

Step 3: Count the total number of nouns

Cloud	Grass	Happy
Sun	Flower	Eat
Umbrella	Quickly	Rain
Shoes	Butterflies	Running

Total number of nouns: _____

Story Time

Complete the story with the help of the words in the Help Box.

Help Box

| elder sister | pet | parents | Sunday | sandwiches |
| fruits | juices | swim | ball | |

On _____ we are going on a picnic. I am going with my _____ and _____. We will take our _____ dog along with us. We will pack lots of _____, _____ and _____. We will play with a _____ and go for a _____ in the pool.

117 From A to Z

Arrange these toys in an alphabetical order.

Help Box

doll	toy car	robot
cricket ball	football	chess
kite	snakes and ladder	monopoly
tennis racket		

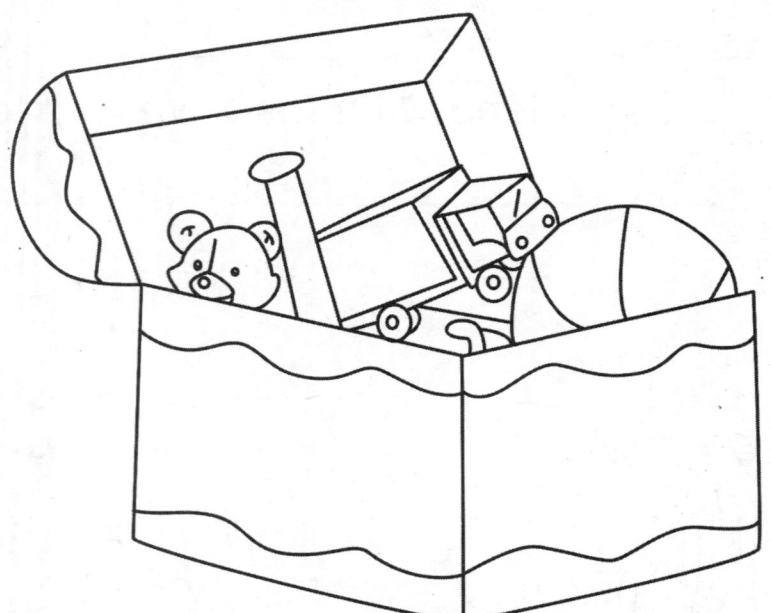

Alphabetisation

Write the words in each row in an alphabetical order.

LIVE	SO	JUST	ANY
_____	_____	_____	_____

OPEN	TOP	DUCK	GIVE
_____	_____	_____	_____

WALK	TALK	CAN	MAN
_____	_____	_____	_____

PIN	CHAIN	APPLE	GOAT
_____	_____	_____	_____

OLD	NEW	PARROT	HOUSE
_____	_____	_____	_____

Date: _____   Teacher's Signature: _____

119 Guess the Name

Guess the name of the activity in the picture. _____

Categorise it as:

Boring ☐

Adventurous ☐

In One Word

Use one word (an adjective) to describe the picture. One of them has been done for you.

Hot

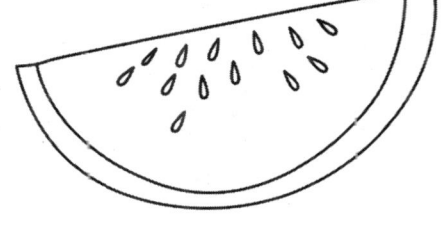

_____

_____   _____

_____   _____

Date: _____   Teacher's Signature: _____

121 Peek-A-Boo!

Look at the pictures given below and draw a line to match each animal with its habitat.

'E' and 'J'

Each picture here starts with either the letter 'E' or with 'J'. Fill in the blanks with the appropriate word taking help from pictures.

1. When the weather is cold, a _____ keeps you warm.

2. The number _____ comes after ten.

3. _____ or Jam are kept in a glass _____.

4. We use an _____ to remove the pencil marks.

5. The _____ and the _____ are the organs to see and hear.

Two or Too?

Two is a number, while too means also. Choose the correct one of them and complete the sentence.

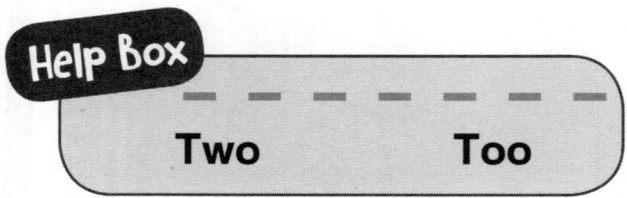

Mr Tom has _____ children. One is Charlie and other Maria.

Alex is a carpenter. He can make, table, chair and bed, _____.

Shelly has _____ pets, Mixy and Teddy.

Papia has a big car, a small car and a truck, _____.

It's Mother's Day!

What does 'mother' mean to you? Write a word for each alphabet and then write a few sentences about your mother.

M
O
T
H
E
R

Date: _____   Teacher's Signature: _____

125 Let's Write

Look at the picture given below and answer the questions.

Where is this happening? _____

Who are there in the above picture? _____

What is happening in the picture? _____

Date: _____ Teacher's Signature: _____

I Am Letter 'C'

How much do you know about letter 'C'? Match the following.

Candy

Cactus

Coconut Tree

Carrot

Candle

Coat

Cloud

Camera

Date: _____ Teacher's Signature: _____

127 Colour and Know!

Colour the picture given below. In which country do people wear this outfit? You can get help from your parents for this one.

Country: _____

Date: _____
Teacher's Signature: _____

It's My Family

What is a family? Write a word for each letter and then make a sentence that defines the meaning of a family for you. Colour the picture of the family, too.

_____

_____

F _____

A _____

M _____

I _____

L _____

Y _____

Date: _____   Teacher's Signature: _____

Five Senses

129

Read the words given in the box and group them according to the five senses of our body: hearing, smell, taste, sight and touch.

Help Box

fragrant	smooth	stinky	sticky
aroma	bells	ugly	sweet
rough	bitter	scenic	drums
thunder	clouds		

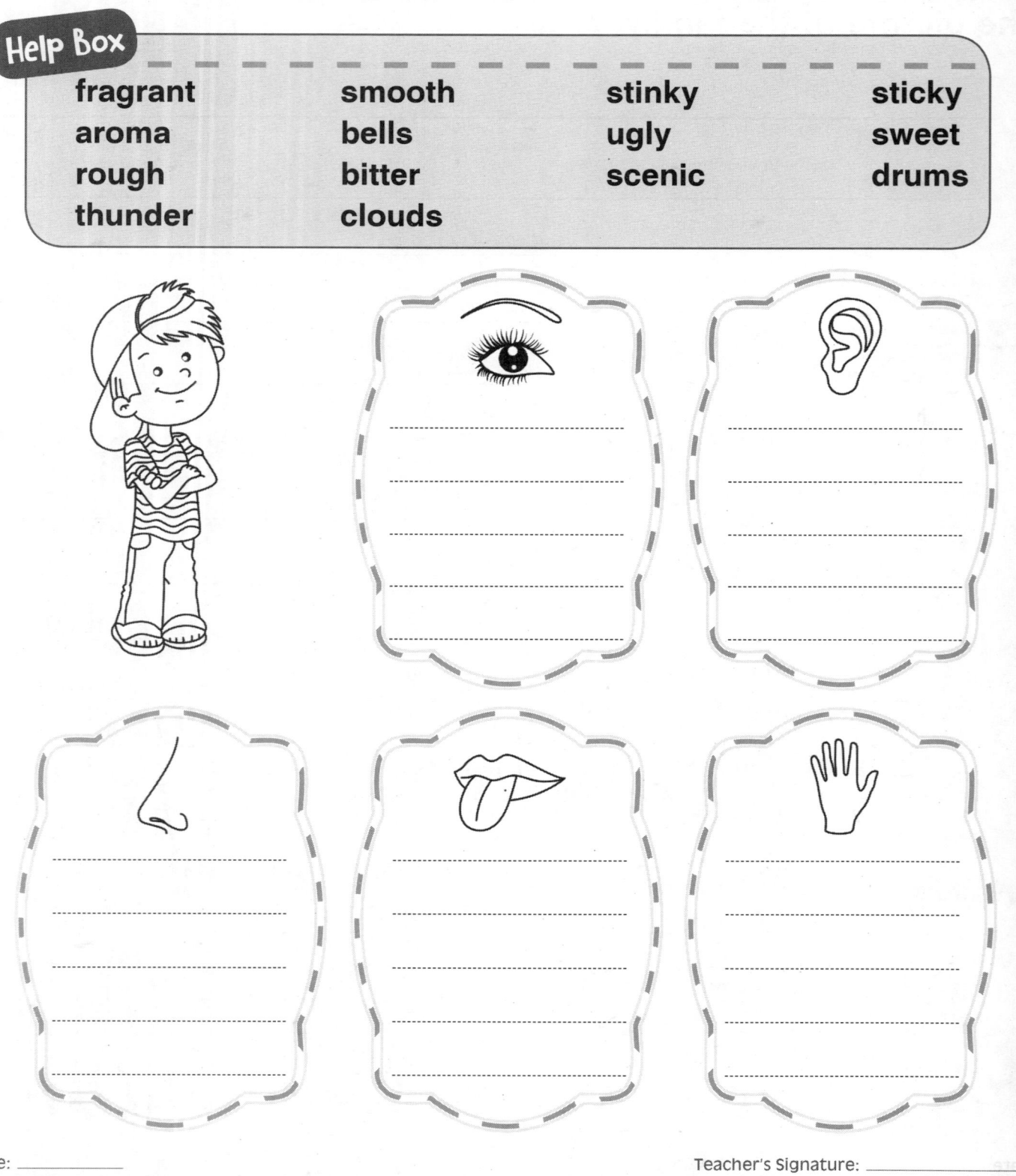

Cow's Act

Match the pictures with the sentence that describes the scene.

the cow acts

the cow sings.

the cow dances

131 Word End

Fill the two missing letters at the end of each word and complete it. Colour the pictures that end with the same letter.

HOR __ __

DRE __ __

KI __ __

LO __ __

COCON __ __

CLO __ __

PEAN __ __

Build a House

Here are pictures of people who help build a house. Identify and write their professions.

_____

_____

_____

_____

Date: _____   Teacher's Signature: _____

133 Similar Letters

Identify the given pictures and find out two common letters in each word and circle them.

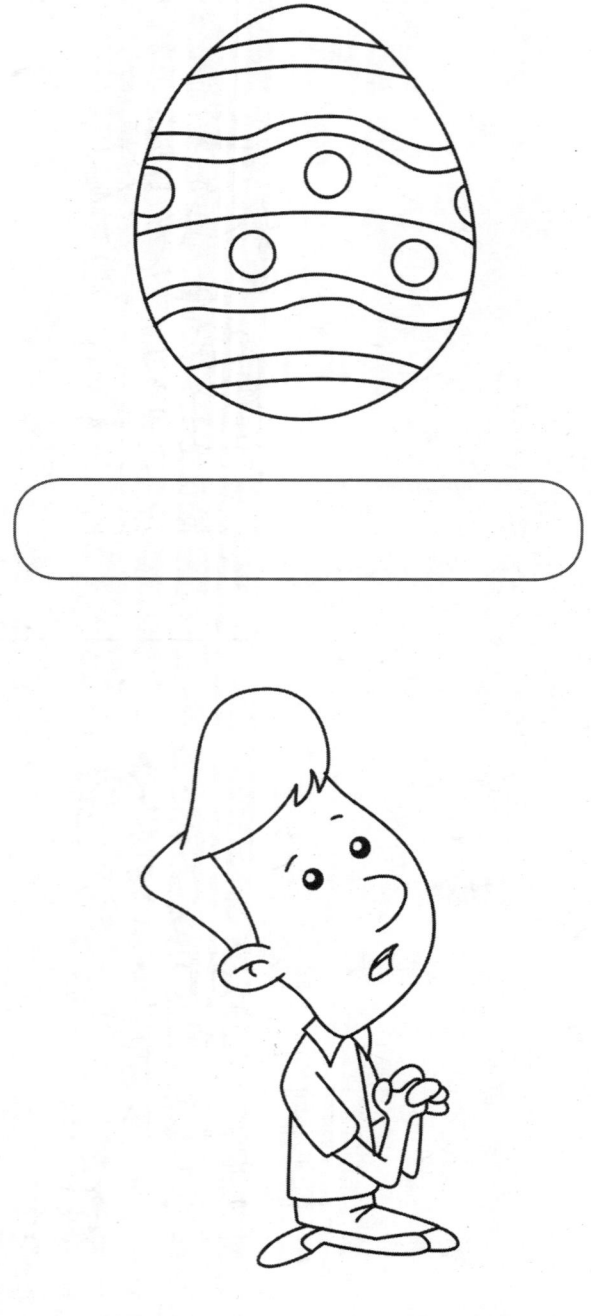

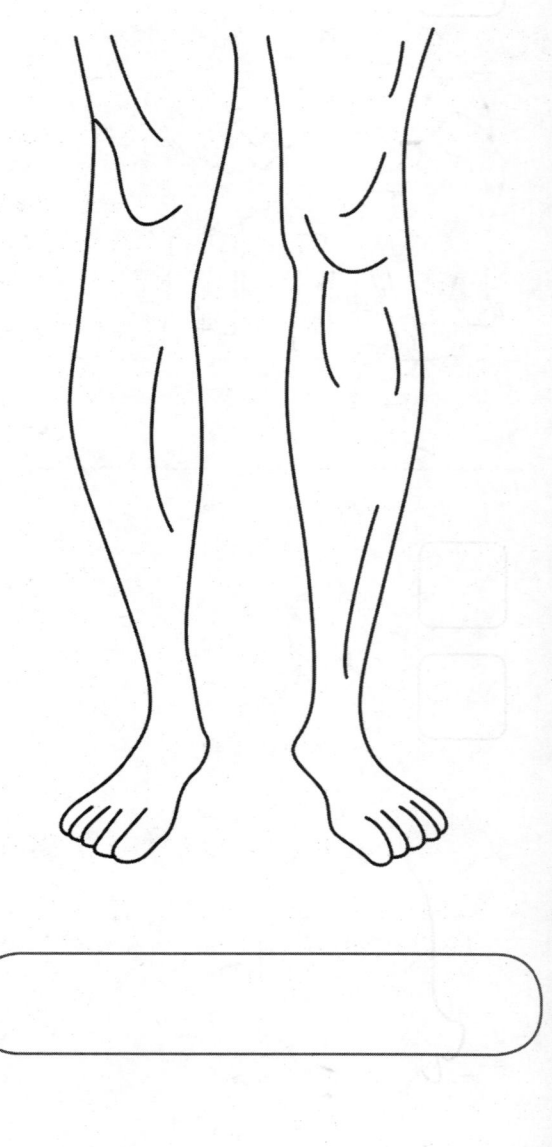

Point of View

What is happening in the pictures? Tick (✓) the sentence that suits the picture.

☐ The cat is sleeping peacefully.
☐ The cat is having a bad dream.

☐ Rain helps the flower grow.
☐ The flowers will not grow.

☐ The boy is eating a sandwich.
☐ The sandwich stained the boy's shirt.

☐ The girl is surprised.
☐ The girl is sad.

135 Things From My Classroom

Unscramble the words and write the correct word.

 PCLIEN _____

 GBA _____

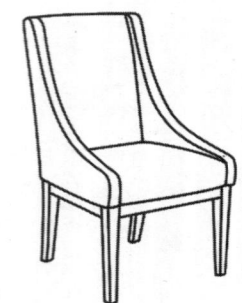 RCHIA _____

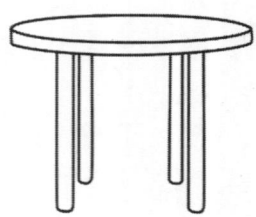 ETABL _____

 ARDBO _____

136 Lost Animals in the Grid

Find the names of the animals given in the Clue Box in the word grid.

Clue Box

Donkey	Sheep	Horse	Cow	Goat
Ox	Pig	Camel	Buffalo	

N	N	P	U	L	Z	G	Y	Z	L
S	J	I	F	J	H	O	R	S	E
Y	C	G	I	O	K	A	D	S	S
D	O	N	K	E	Y	T	V	S	Q
X	W	G	A	E	O	I	C	H	T
B	U	F	F	A	L	O	A	E	N
W	L	E	N	R	R	H	M	E	D
D	I	J	S	N	I	L	E	P	E
W	Q	A	K	R	R	Q	L	Z	P
X	B	G	O	X	Y	V	K	I	E

Date: _____ Teacher's Signature: _____

137 Santa Emoticons

Look at the four different pictures of Santa. Write one word to describe the expression in each picture.

Spot the Difference

Do the two pictures look the same? They are not! Find 3 differences.

139 Words in the Picture

Read the words in the box and circle the things related to these words in the picture.

Sun	Christmas tree	Stars
Mat	Glasses	Plates
Basket	Ball	Man
Children	Wind	Grass

The A,B,C Words

Complete the missing letters in the words, they mainly start with A, B and C. Match the pictures with the words.

   _ _ O K

   _ IR _

   _ P P _ _

   _ _ R T

   _ _ L L O _ _

   _ A _

   _ _ K E

141 The Right One

Choose the correct option to complete the sentences.

1. Jim plays _____ (outdoor/indoor) games.

2. The leaves of that tree are_____ (falling/growing).

3. Rony likes _____ (fur/wollen) coat.

4. The pilot flies a _____ (helicopter/fighter jet)

142   Letters in a Curl

Form correct adjectives from the letters in the curly triangles that suit the words given below. The first one has been done for you.

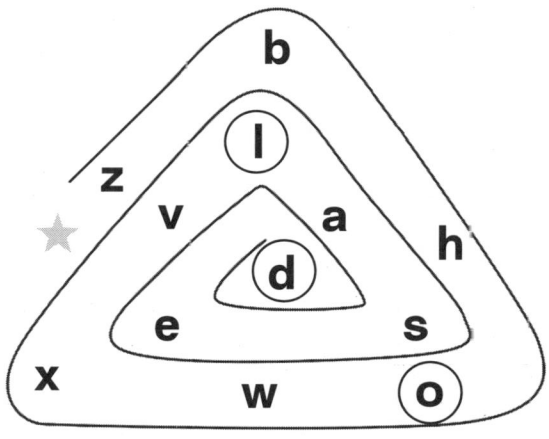

Old

GRANDFATHER

1

WINTER

2

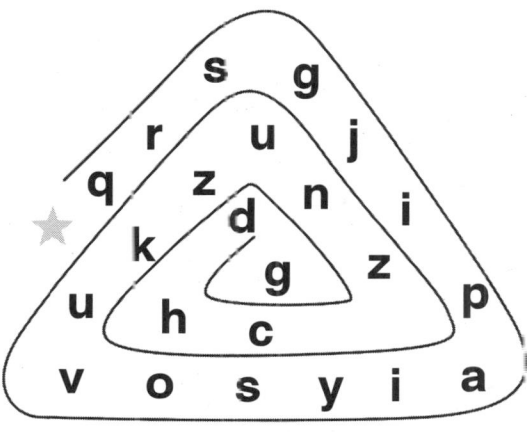

WORM

3

Fruit Crossword

Look at the picture clues and complete the crossword.

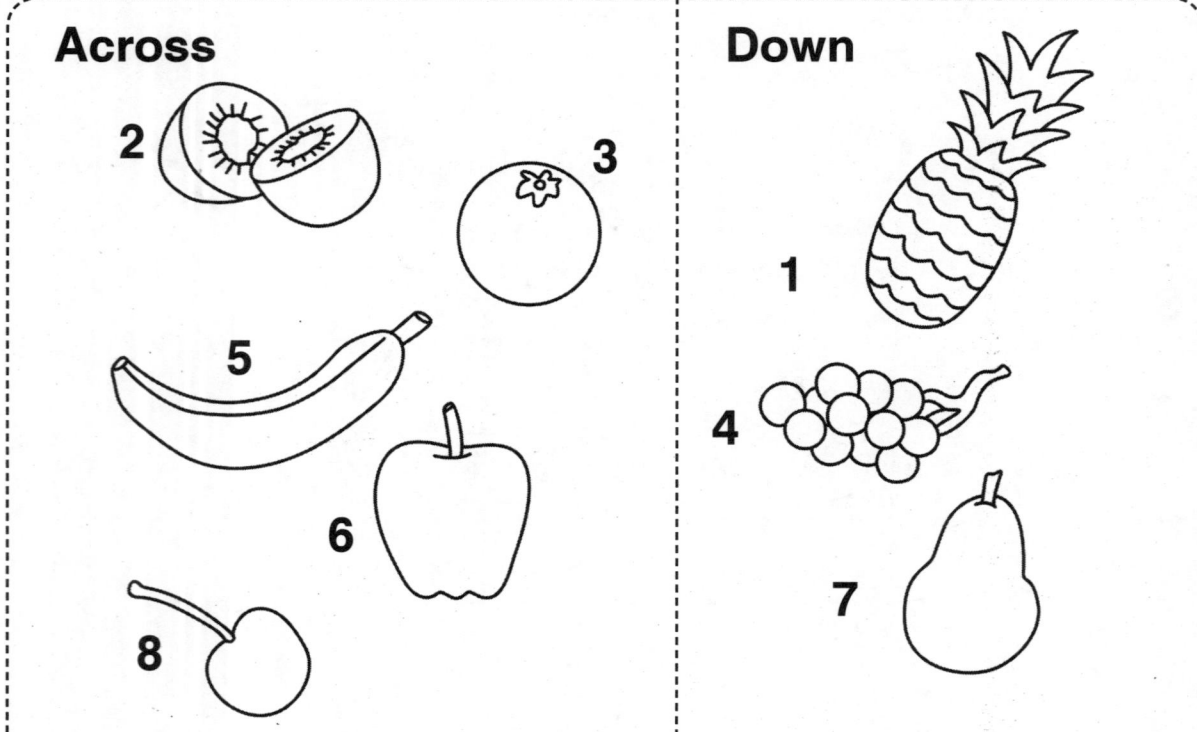

Across: 2, 3, 5, 6, 8

Down: 1, 4, 7

One-Word Play

Circle the letter that will change the meaning of the words in each row. The picture will provide the clue on which letter should be changed. The first row has been done for you.

B(a)d Boy

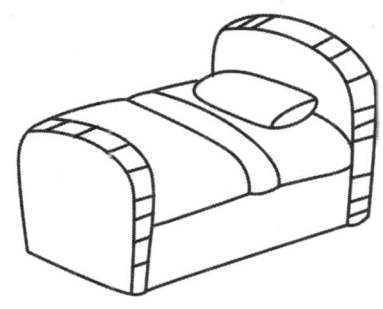

Small B(e)d

School Bag

Big Whale

Black Cat

Baby Cot

145 Sounds I Make

Match the living beings with the sounds they make.

'Bow wow', says the dog.

'Mew mew', says the cat.

Bleat bleat', says the goat.

Roar roar', says the lion.

'Hello, hello', says the child.

We Work in Pairs

Match the following to make pairs. The first one has been done for you.

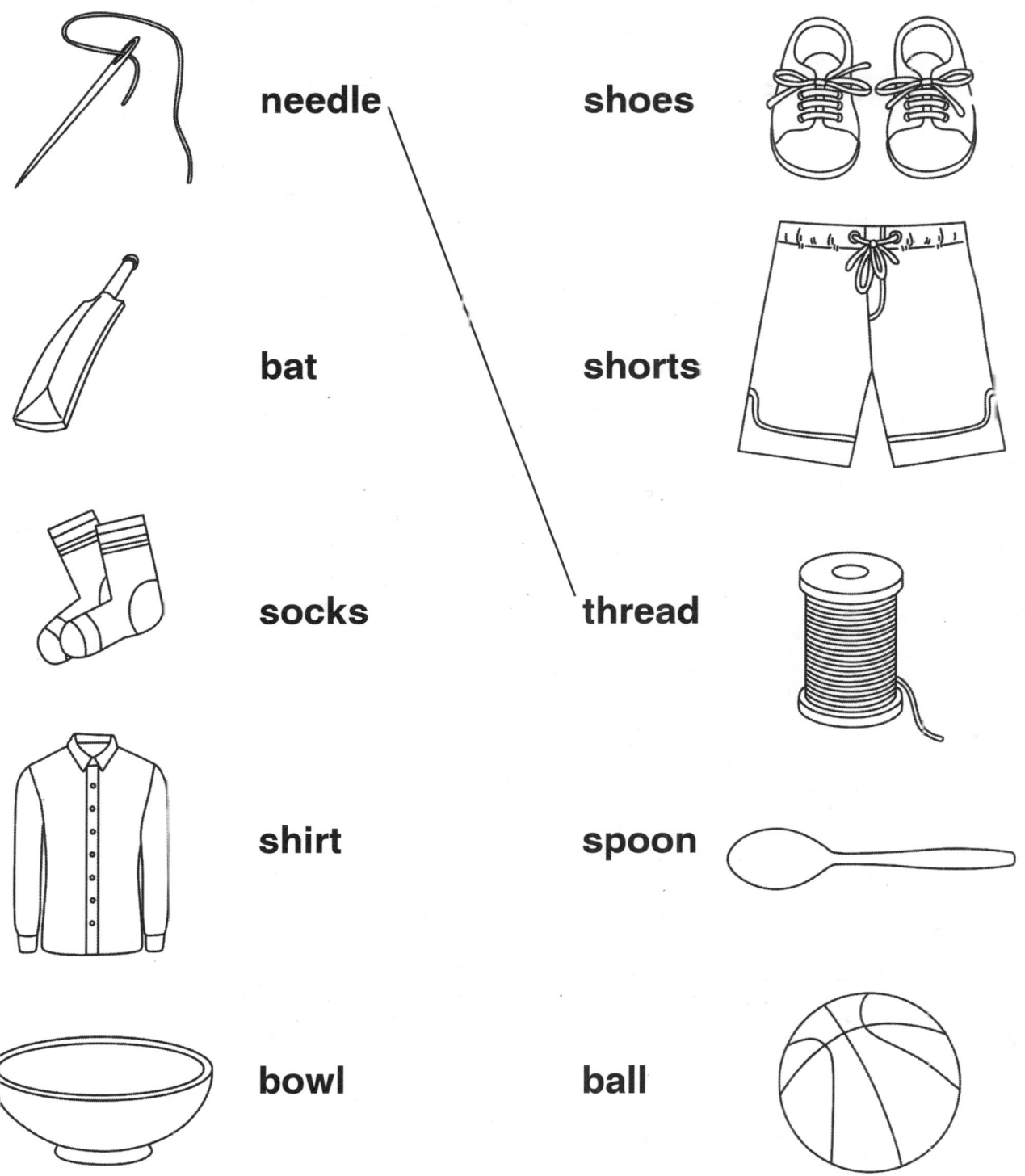

147 Sink or Float?

Take a tub of water and put the things given here in it one by one. Write 'S' for objects that sink in water and write 'F' for objects that float in water.

You can get help from your parents or an elder sibling to collect the material.

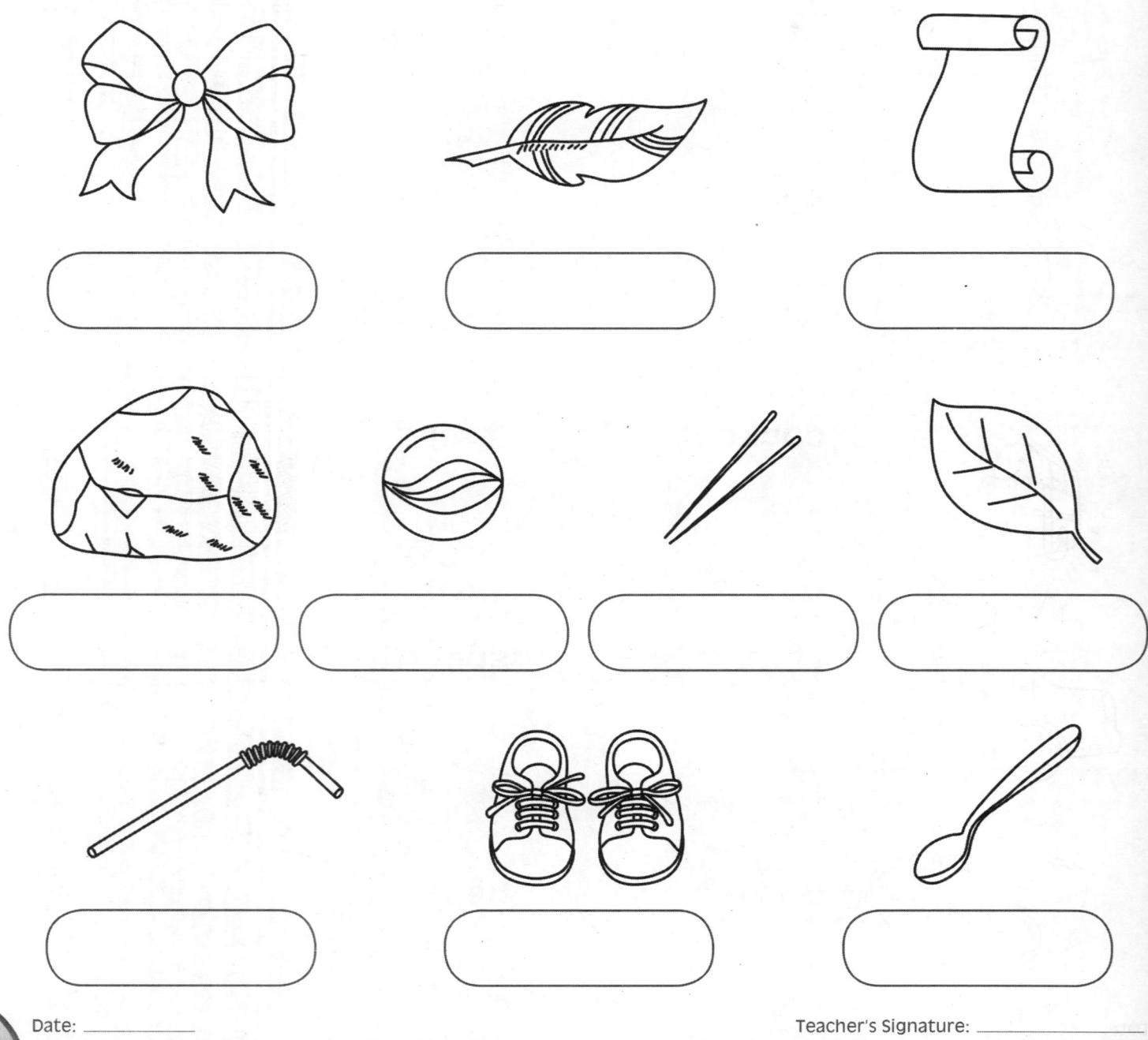

Vroom!

Identify the vehicles and match with the pictures.

   Bus

   Airplane

   Ambulance

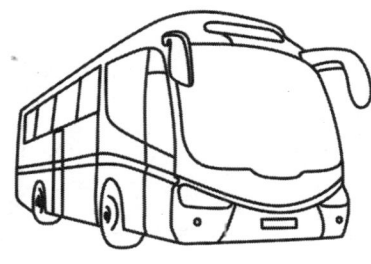   Motorbike

   Bicycle

   Car

149 Find My Name

Look at the pictures given below. Choose the appropriate names for each picture.

City   Iguana   Baker   Globe   Antelope   Judge

150 I Love My Park

Nancy is playing in a park but she doesn't know the names of the various rides in the park. Help her by labelling them.

| Monkey Bars | Slide | Trampoline | See-saw | Net |

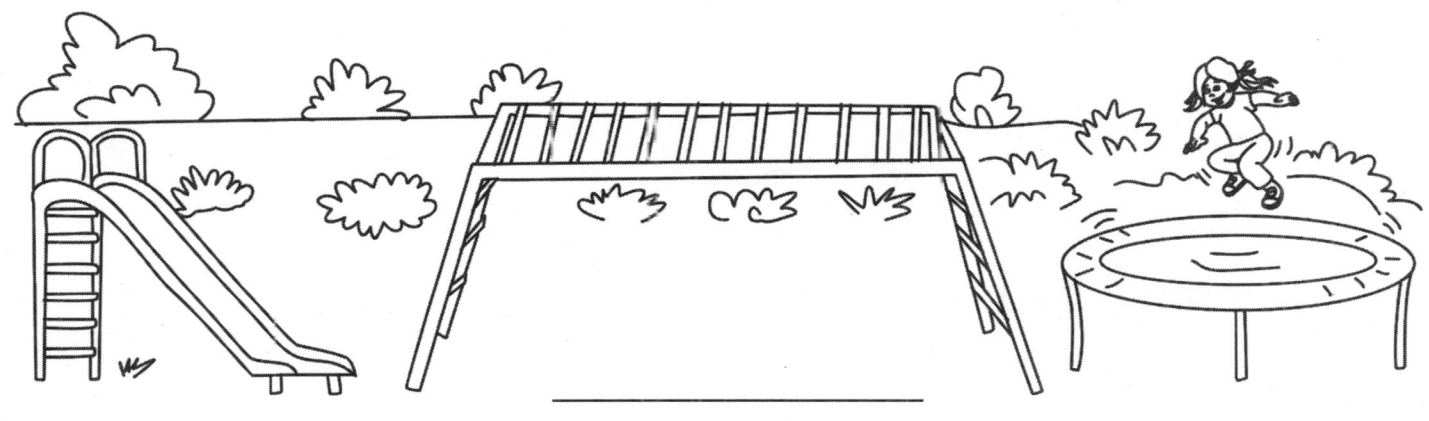

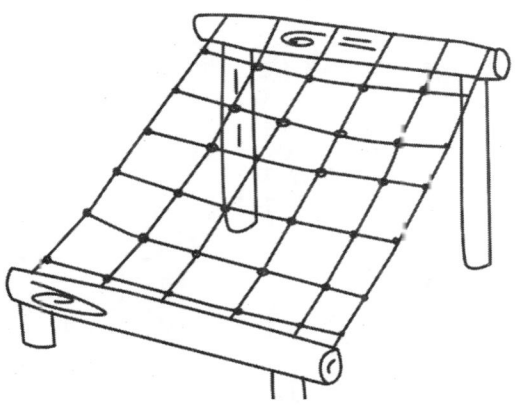

151 We Are Opposites

Match each word with its opposite.

BIG   OLD

WEAK   NARROW

BEAUTIFUL   DRY

WIDE   STRONG

WET   SMALL

YOUNG   UGLY

Same-Same

Match the words that have the same meaning.

BIG	BROAD
BEAUTIFUL	MOIST
WEAK	PRETTY
WIDE	YOUTHFUL
WET	FRAGILE
YOUNG	LARGE

153 Animal Search Engine

Mark the domestic animals with blue pen, wild animals with red pen and pet animals with green pen in the given word maze.

E	L	L	P	T	X	P	P	I	K	T	T	J
X	T	B	E	A	R	K	D	N	D	P	I	J
H	O	R	S	E	L	I	O	N	H	A	G	E
M	D	E	X	P	W	O	L	F	M	R	E	S
R	E	D	R	P	E	Z	P	D	A	R	R	H
J	I	O	R	J	H	K	H	L	N	O	R	A
I	A	G	G	A	L	L	I	G	A	T	O	R
C	E	A	T	D	M	Z	N	I	T	D	H	K
Q	R	A	B	B	I	T	K	F	E	I	M	O
W	F	M	R	P	A	N	T	H	E	R	E	N
U	Z	T	C	O	W	S	D	L	X	X	B	Y

Help Box

ALLIGATOR	BEAR	COW	DOG
DOLPHIN	HORSE	LION	MANATEE
PANTHER	PARROT	RABBIT	SHARK
TIGER	WOLF		

Date: _____   Teacher's Signature: _____

154 Describe the Scene

Match the sentences with the correct scene.

Children are playing in a park.

This child has curly hair.

The man is lifting heavy weight.

Two children are fighting.

155 Letter Hexagon

Make four new words using letters given in the hexagon. The letter in the centre should be present in all the new words.

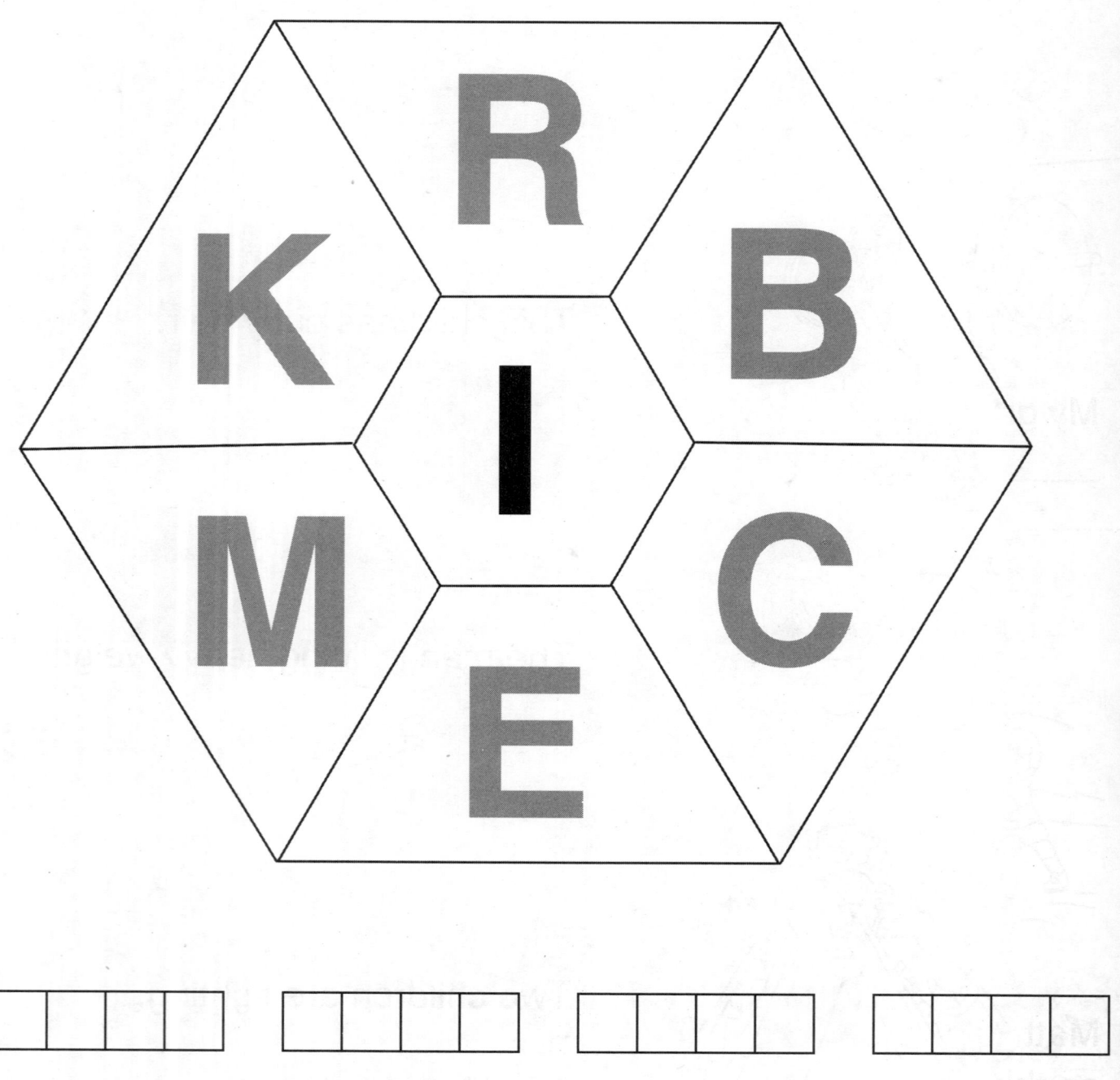

And or But?

Add 'and' or 'but' whichever is correct, in the sentences to complete them.

(and, but)

My grandma makes tasty food _____ tasty snacks.

(and, but)

Her writing is good _____ her spellings are weak.

(and, but)

Matt _____ John are playing on the beach.

(and, but)

Alice fell down _____ she did not get hurt.

Daily Needs

Fill in the blanks with correct option.

1. We use _____ to clean our ears.

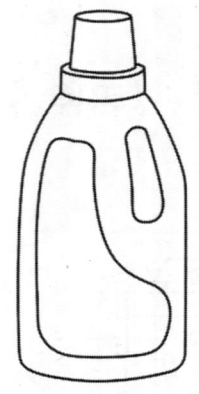 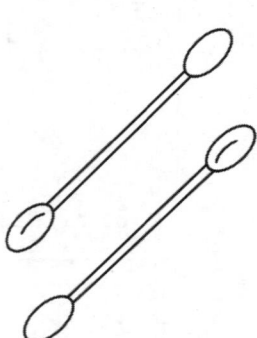 

Detergents   **Cotton buds**   **Toothpaste**

2. We use a _____ to keep our hair neat and tidy.

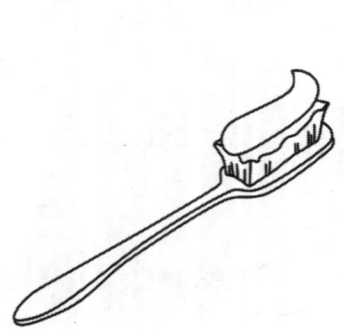 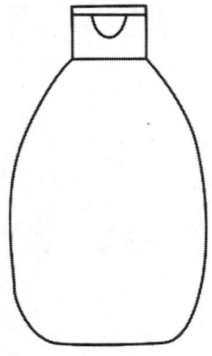 

Toothbrush   **Shampoo**   **Hair brush**

We Sound the Same!

When two words have different meanings and spellings but sound the same, they are called homophones. Pick such words from the Help Box to complete the activity.

Help Box

SUM   BEAN   PEACE   BY   TWO   WAIT   HARE   ROLL

Some →	SUM	Role →	ROLL
Piece →	PEACE	Bye →	BY
To →	TWO	Been →	BEAN
Hair →	HARE	Weight →	WAIT

Crooked Sentence

Rearrange the following words to make meaningful sentences.

1. hot the sun is very

   _____

2. bought new dress yesterday I a

   _____

3. not the do clothes boy fit the

   _____

4. will not school go I to tomorrow

   _____

5. my hair ties grandma my every day

   _____

He or She?

Complete the sentences given below with 'He' or 'She'.

_____ is drinking juice.

_____ is going to school.

161 'A' or 'An'?

Look at the pictures and read the sentences. Tick (✓) the correct answer.

1. I would love to eat a/an apple.

2. My father gave me an/a present.

3. The girl is riding a/an bicycle.

 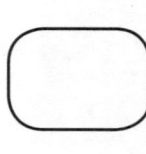

4. Julie kept a/an orange on the table.

Date: _____   Teacher's Signature: _____

Letter Game for Two

Write a word starting with the letters given below on a piece of paper. It's a two-player game. Take turns to come up with the words. The one who cannot write a correct word looses a point.

START   **FINISH**

A, e, T, s, X, W, F, Q, d, H, m, J, M, L, Y, i, U, D

163 Pictionary

Identify the pictures by using the words from the Help Box.

Help Box
Back   pack   Sack   Rack   Snack   Stack   Quack

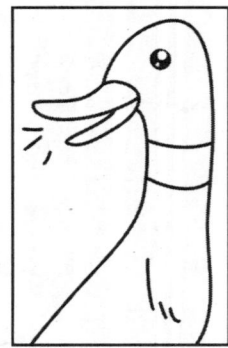 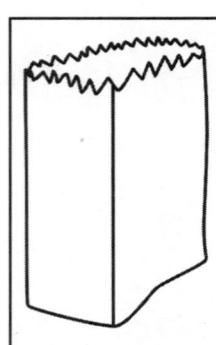  

_____   _____   _____   _____

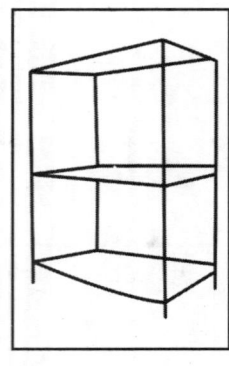 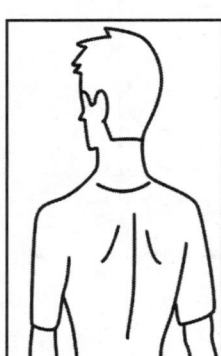 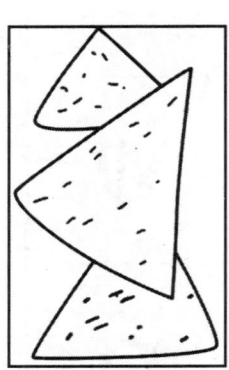

_____   _____   _____

Identify the three letters that are common in all the words.
___, ___ and ___

Date: _____   Teacher's Signature: _____

164 That Describes Me Best

Choose one word each from the box to describe the pictures.

bricks

sucker

cactus

feather

potatoes

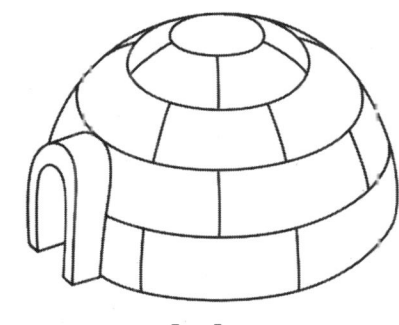
Igloo

thumbtack

squirrel

cold
hard
sticky
furry
sharp
lumpy
light
prickly

165 Punctuation Riddle

Use the correct punctuation mark to fill in the blanks.
Full stop (.), Exclamation mark (!), or Question mark (?)

1. The bus is red _____

2. Where is the horse _____

3. I love chocolates _____

4. What is the time in your clock _____

5. You are great _____

6. Cats like milk _____

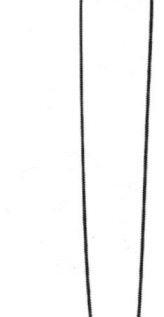

166 Replace and Rewrite

Replace the underlined word with the options given below each sentence. Now, rewrite the sentence in the blank space.

My dog's paws are large!

giant   small   big

This pillow feels cozy and soft.

fluffy   hard   comfy

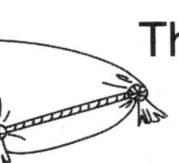

She is happy today!

glad   sad   joyful

The bird flew up in the air.

down   high   right

Date: _____   Teacher's Signature: _____

Before or After?

Fill in the blanks by adding either 'before' or 'after' and complete the sentences.

Lunch is _____ breakfast.

11 am comes _____ 10 am.

10 comes _____ 11

11 comes _____ 12

Z comes _____ X.

L comes _____ N

168 African Safari

Find the names of the animals that live in the African savannah in the word grid.

Names are given in the box.

LION	ELEPHANT	HIPPO	RHINO
GIRAFFE	HYENA	ZEBRA	CHIMP

Y	W	O	K	F	Z	Q	F	B	W
C	H	I	M	P	R	H	I	N	O
W	I	O	W	B	L	I	O	N	M
O	P	Z	Z	E	B	R	A	I	O
E	P	L	N	Q	M	B	H	D	Z
W	O	Z	Q	H	M	R	Y	W	B
Y	R	J	S	D	F	B	E	E	C
C	E	L	E	P	H	A	N	T	P
M	A	Z	L	N	R	H	A	U	A
B	Z	C	G	I	R	A	F	F	E

Date: _____ Teacher's Signature: _____

169 Blast from the Past

This picture belongs to the Ancient Egypt. Look for a real photograph of Ancient Egyptian civilization and colour this picture with similar colours.

Get help from your parents to find the picture.

Explain About Me

For example: Jim has a beautiful house. The word 'beautiful' is an adjective for the word 'house'. Now, match the given nouns with suitable adjectives.

Nouns	Adjectives
Cat	Red
Hotel	Noisy
Table	Loving
Teacher	Smart
Mother	Big
Apple	Smelly
Chair	Hairy
Shoe	Wooden
Television	Huge

171 It's Playtime

Write the names of three famous people from the following sports in the empty boxes.

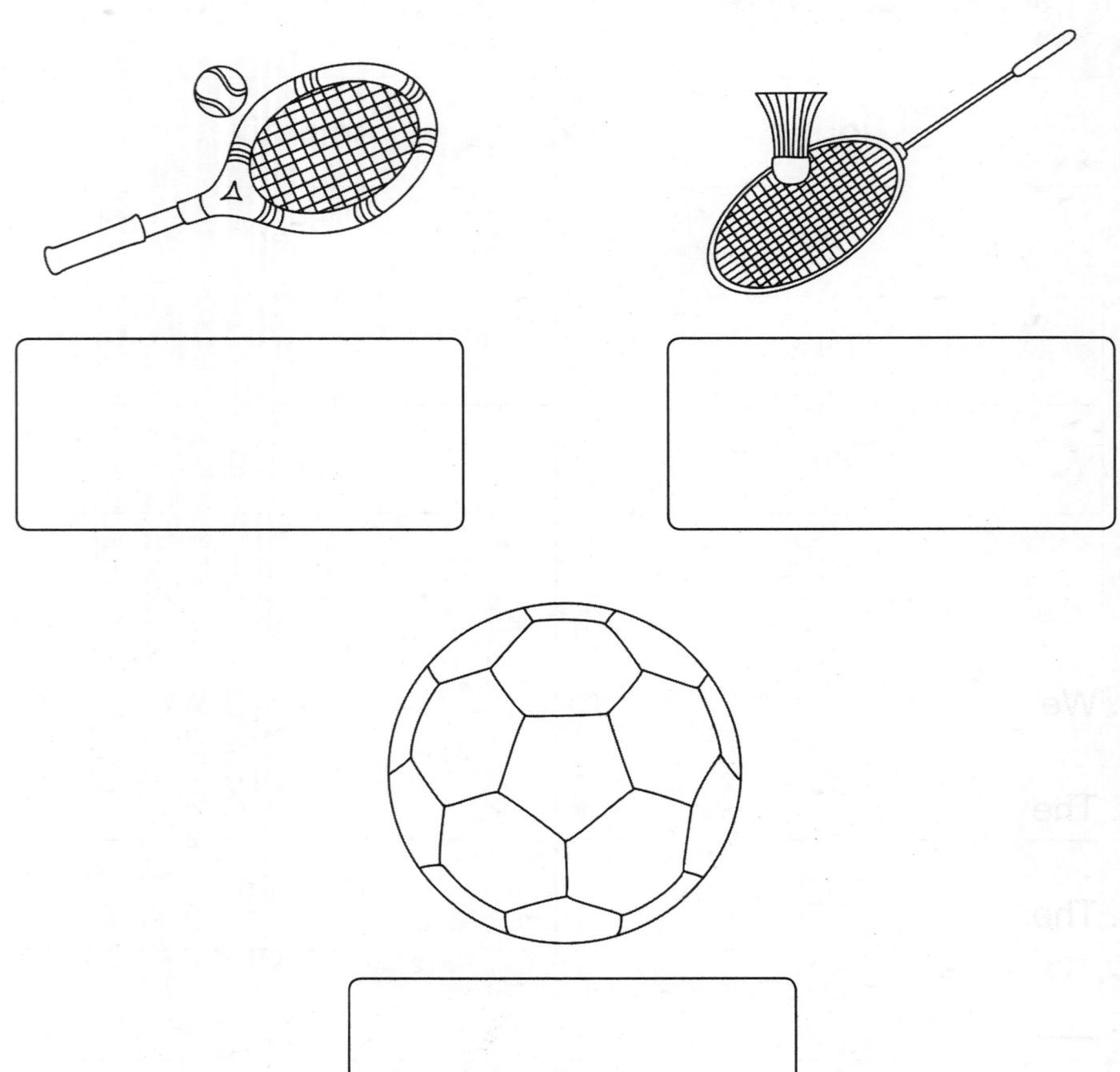

Space Connection

Complete the sentences.

1. We see sun, moon and stars in the _____.

2. The _____ shines during the day.

3. The _____ shines in the night.

4. _____ are of different sizes.

5. _____ appears only in night.

Date: _____   Teacher's Signature: _____

173   I Feel...

Draw any three emotions on the blank faces and write the word that describes the emotion under each picture.

Help Box

Happy   Sad   Angry

_____

_____

_____

Date: _____   Teacher's Signature: _____

174 Water Drop

Select the best three words for the blanks in the poem and complete it.

Help Box

bath   wash   plants   animals   swim

Water to Drink

Water to _____

Water to _____

Water to _____

Life without water

I don't think.

Date: _____   Teacher's Signature: _____

175 The Chase!

Imagine what this mouse and cat are saying to each other. Write the dialogues in the space below each picture.

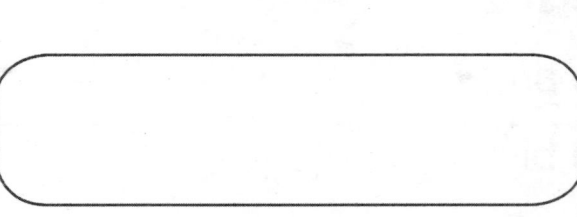

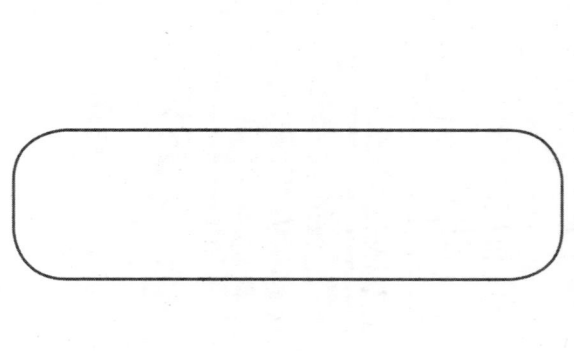

Date: _____   Teacher's Signature: _____

What's Happening?

Tick (✓) the sentence that describes the picture.

The small boy is wearing a small shirt.
The small boy is wearing a big shirt.
The big boy is wearing a torn shirt.

This leaf is diamond-shaped.
This leaf is heart-shaped.
This leaf is square-shaped.

A happy boy is walking with an excited dog.
A happy boy is walking with a black dog.
A happy boy is walking with two dogs.

177 Things in the Picture

Colour the picture of the beach that you see below using your imagination.

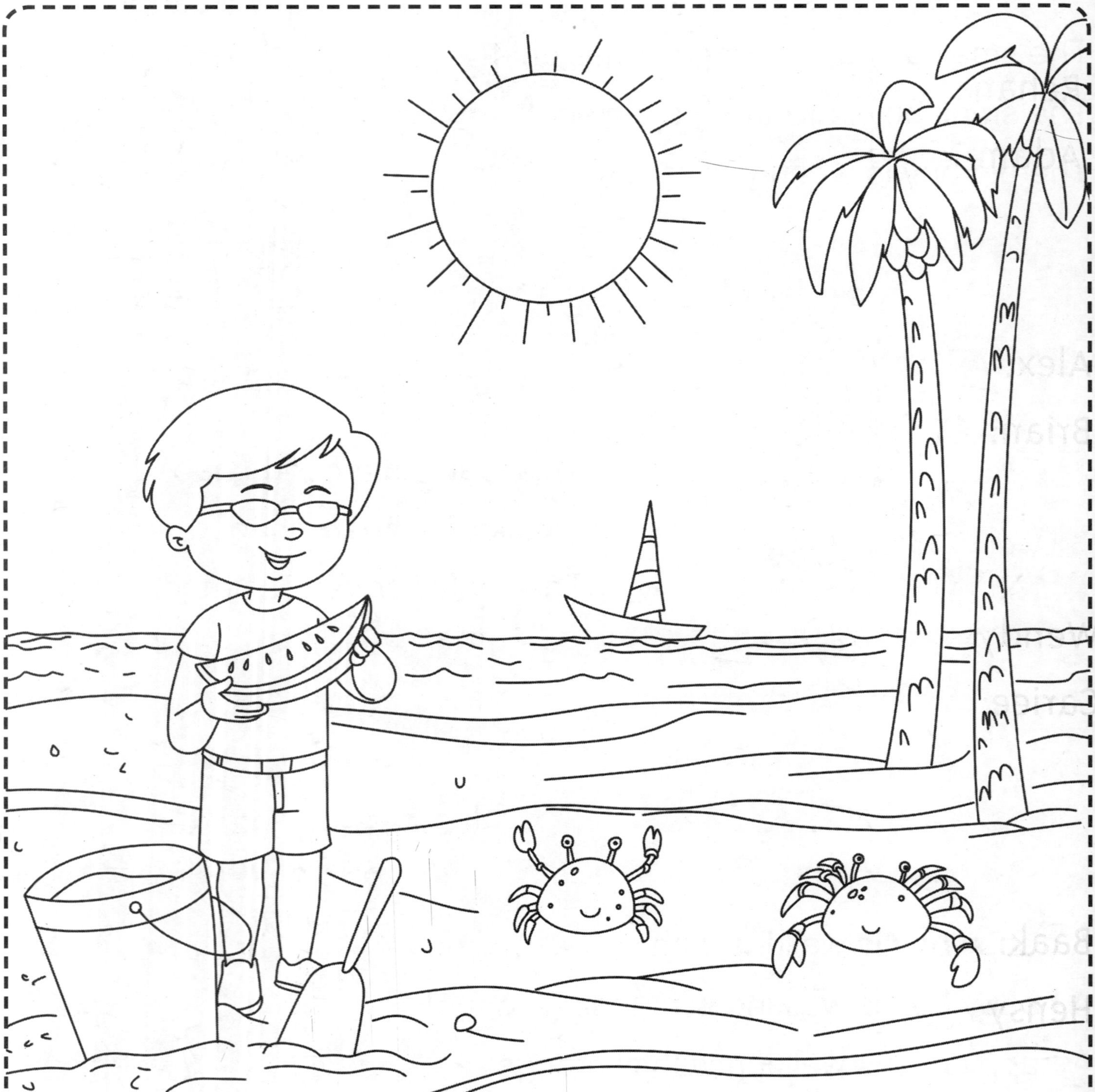

Date: ____________ Teacher's Signature: ____________

Who Is Right?

Look at the picture and read the sentences. Choose the correct sentences. Write the name of the child who is right.

Rehana: A calendar is under the wall

Adam: A calendar is on the wall

Who is right: ⬚

Alex: A spider is in its web.

Brian: A spider is under its web.

Who is right: ⬚

Wendy: A lion is in the zoo.

Cariee: A lion is under the zoo.

Who is right: ⬚

Baak: A kite is on the stool.

Hensy: A kite is in under the stool.

Who is right: ⬚

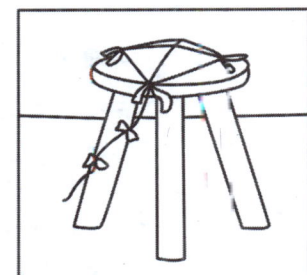

In, On or Under?

Look at the pictures and choose their position. Circle the correct answer.

Position of eggs:

(in, on, under)

Position of jug:

(in, on, under)

Position of girl:

(in, on, under)

Position of bear:

(in, on, under)

Date: _____   Teacher's Signature: _____

In Action

Action words are the words that describe an action in a sentence. For example: A boy is playing. 'Playing' is an action so 'playing' is the action word.

Circle the action words among following words.

Throw	Shoe
Tree	Dance
Sing	Balloon
Walk	Pick
Fruit	Paper
Shout	Umbrella

Date: _____ Teacher's Signature: _____

181 Things on a Tree

Circle the things that you find on a tree.

beehive

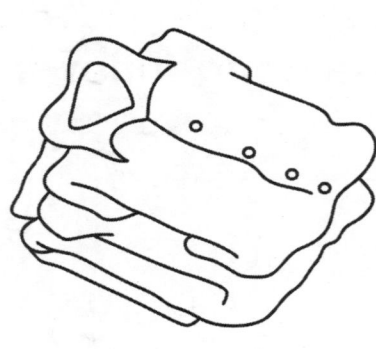
clothes

kite

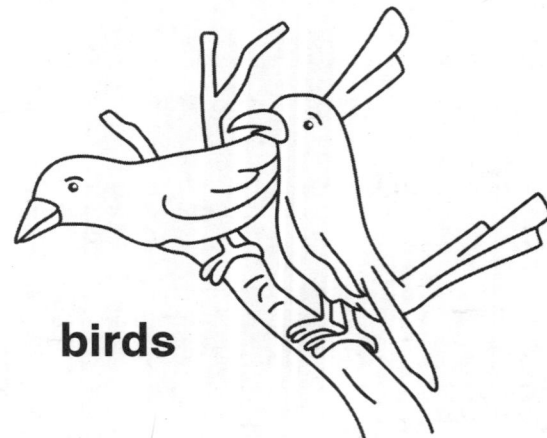
birds

pencil

leaves

ant

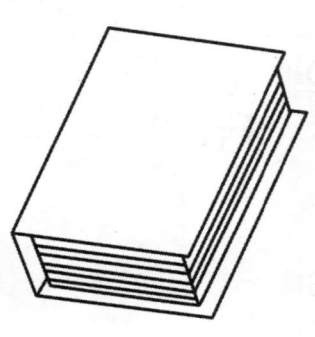
book

A Baby's Dream

Check the spelling errors in the highlighted words and correct them.

The little berds had gone to bed, _____

The fiches all came out to play, _____

The snowdraup lifted high its head, _____

The emu and the kangaru, _____

Were eating strawbarries and cream ; _____

The picock sang a song to woo _____

The snow-white swaan, in Baby's dream. _____

Date: _____ Teacher's Signature: _____

183 Right Match

Choose one heading each for the pictures from the Help Box.

Help Box
Crossing Road   My Favourite toys   In the Zoo   I love books

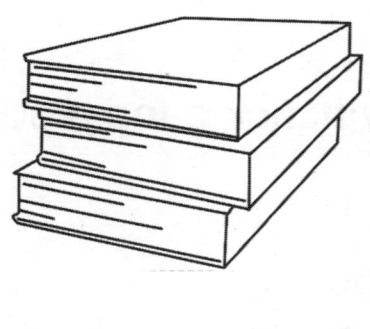

I or Me?

Use either 'I' or 'me' correctly to complete the sentences.

1. _____ have a pet turtle.

2. Hand _____ the hammer.

3. Mom and _____ washed the windows.

4. My friend gave _____ a present.

5. Would you like to come with _____ ?

6. _____ had fun at the zoo.

185 The Bee and Her Home!

Little Bee forgot the way to her home. Help her find her way home.

Words on My Back!

Help the bumble bees unscramble the word on her wings. The answers will be the opposite of the word given on the left.

1. up 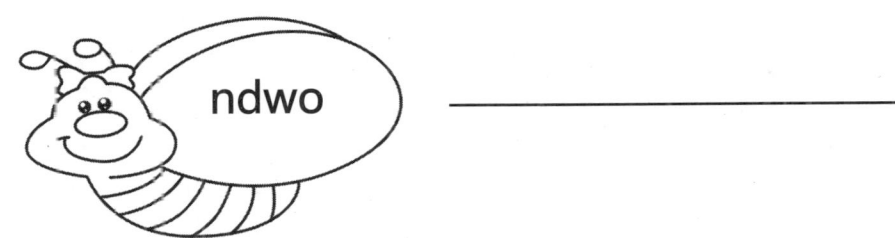 _____

2. big 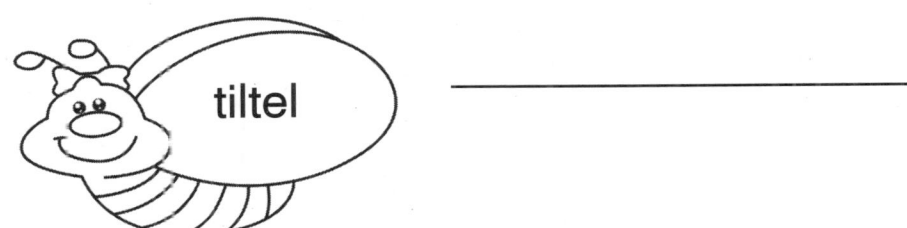 _____

3. cry 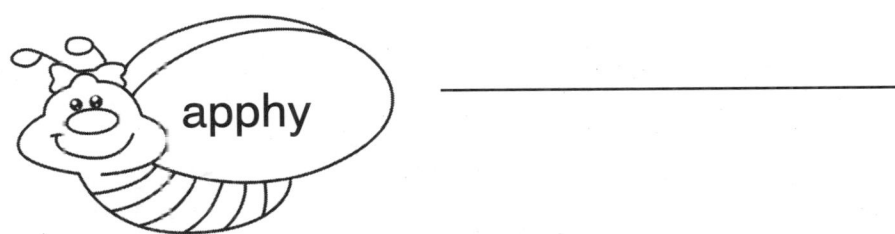 _____

4. go 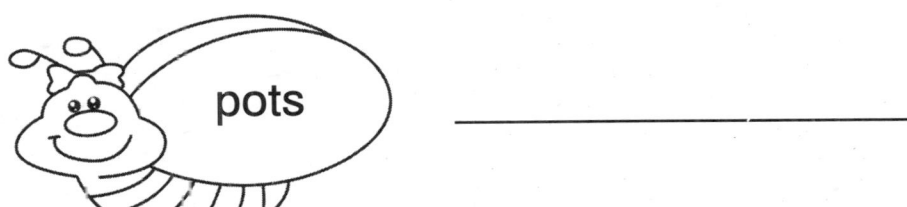 _____

5. short 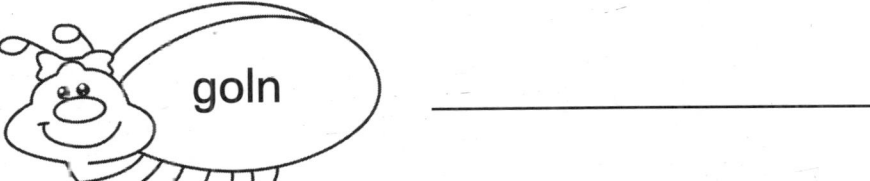 _____

Date: _____ Teacher's Signature: _____

187 Matching pairs

Circle the matching pair of words with same colour.

this   he   fee
      that
See   hat   this
      sea
                on
gone   sit   from

      well   con   son
came

      set   soon   ate
gone
      form
   eat   well   Home

Mixed up Rhyme

Do you know the nursery rhyme Jack and Jill? Now, write the rhyme in correct order.

Jack fell down, And broke his crown

And Jill came tumbling after.

Jack and Jill, Went up the hill

To fetch a pail of water.

189 What Am I Doing?

Circle the part of the sentence that shows the work or action that is happening in the picture. The first one has been done for you.

The firemen (pull the hose.)

The clown juggled the balls.

The baby swims in the pool.

The clown rides a unicycle.

The children sing.

Search and Draw

Follow the instructions.

1. Find something that begins with the same sound as <u>run</u>.

   Draw a picture of it.

   Find something that begins with the same sound as <u>ball</u>.

   Draw a picture of it.

2. Find something that ends with the same sound as <u>wet</u>.

   Draw a picture of it.

   Find something that ends with the same sound as <u>good</u>.

   Draw a picture of it.

Date: _____   Teacher's Signature: _____

191 I Would/ I Wouldn't

Write the name of a person you would or wouldn't...

	Would	Wouldn't
shake hands with		
Play with		
Talk to		

Date: _____

Teacher's Signature: _____